THE JEWISH BASEBALL HALL OF FAME

A Who's Who of Baseball Stars

Erwin Lynn

DEDICATION

To my parents.

To my wife, and children.

—E.L.

A Shapolsky Book
Published by Shapolsky Publishers

Copyright © 1987 by Erwin Lynn

For any additional information, contact:
Shapolsky Publishers, Inc.
56 East 11th Street, NY, NY 10003

10 9 8 7 6 5 4 3 2 1
First Edition April 1987

Library of Congress Cataloging in Publication Data
Lynn, Erwin
The Jewish Baseball Hall of Fame

Bibliography: p.
1. Baseball players—United States—Biography.
2. Jews—United States—Biography.   I. Title

GV865.A1L96   1986   796.357′092′2   [B] 86-60561
ISBN 0-933503-17-2

Some of the quizzes previously appeared, in slightly different form, as the JEWISH BASEBALL QUIZ.
© 1982, 1983, 1984, 1985 by Erwin Lynn Features.

Acknowledgments

I wish to thank the baseball celebrities who shared their time and recollections: Cal Abrams, Bob Berman, Cy Block, Harry Chozen, Andy Cohen, Hy Cohen, Harry Danning, Mike Epstein, Eddie Feinberg, Al Forman, Joe Ginsberg, Izzy Goldstein, Steve Hertz, Ken Holtzman, Ed Mayer, Steve Ratzer, Al Richter, Al Rosen, Goody Rosen, Marv Rotblatt, Mickey Rutner, Richie Scheinblum, Bill Starr, Don Taussig, Phil Weintraub, Ed Wineapple.

Thank you to Mark E. Mishanie whose editorial assistance with parts of this book was immeasurable. Additionally, to The Society For American Baseball Research, especially: Cliff Kachline, Cooperstown, New York, and Robert C. McConnell, Wilmington, Delaware. To the staff of The National Baseball Hall of Fame and Library, especially: W. Lloyd Johnson, Senior Research Associate. To Joseph L. Reichler, Major League Baseball Promotion Corporation. And to Roy Silver, New York City, and Ivan Tillem, New York City.

I have made extensive use of the research facilities available at the New York Public Library and the Libraries of Nassau County, New York, especially, Bethpage, Hicksville, Plainview-Old Bethpage, and Syosset.

Photo Credits: Thank you to the baseball celebrities and major league teams that furnished photographs for this book. And to Lew Lipset, Ted & Eleanor Mishanie, Mark R. Schaffer, and Mrs. Clifford Gross.

I thank Ian Shapolsky, whose suggestions helped bring about the completion of the manuscript. Additionally, to Malcolm Jordan-Robinson, whose editorial efforts transformed the manuscript into the completed book.

—E.L.

INTRODUCTION

Baseball is a game enjoyed year after year through memories and statistics. Jewish players have been involved with professional baseball since its beginnings more than 120 years ago.

In our quizzes, we detail events that occurred, in some instances, over a century ago. Our research and player interviews confirm that baseball does reflect the times in the United States; during the early period, Jewish players often changed their names before embarking on a baseball career; in later years, Jewish players, with outstanding minor league credentials, did not advance to the majors as others of equal stature.

This is a book about baseball players of Jewish heritage. We have included several converts to Judaism and one special situation, Rod Carew, who is married to a Jewish girl, and whose children are being raised Jewish. He is studying Judaism, and although information received from several major league teams says otherwise, his wife indicates, "Rod has not converted to Judaism."

We offer the reader quizzes, biographical stories, statistics and photos. Some or all of which we hope you enjoy.

E.L.

Note:
Throughout this book all Jewish names are in *italics.*

1. ▶ Bill Cox surrendered the fifty-eighth and last home run of the 1938 season to this Tigers Jewish slugger . . . ?

2. ▶ Earl Torgeson was the only runner to score off this pitching hero of the 1959 World Series . . . ?

3. ▶ This Jewish Southern-born Yankee was the major league's first designated hitter . . . ?

4. ▶ While winning his first major league game, *Syd Cohen* surrendered this player's 708th and last American League home run . . . ?

5. ▶ This Cubs Jewish hurler was the winning pitcher of the first game at Pittsburgh's Forbes Field . . . ?

6. ▶ After his playing career ended, this pitcher became known as "The Clown Prince of Baseball" . . . ?

JEWISH BASEBALL NEWS   Special

ARTHRITIS FANS KOUFAX

arthritis, **n.** *Inflammation of a joint or joints.*

This is how the dictionary defines the condition that cut short the career of *Sanford Koufax,* who had one of the most brilliant pitching careers in modern-day baseball, and arguably in his day was the finest pitcher in all baseball.

Consider his record: 4 no-hitters (record), 382-strikeout season (record), over 300 K's in 3 different seasons (record), more than one strikeout per inning pitched entire career (record), 4 World Series wins (he was in 4 Series!), struck out 18 batters in 2 different games, 40 shutouts, led league in lowest ERA 5 seasons in a row, 3-time Cy Young winner (1963, '65 and '66), Baseball Writers Most Valuable Player ('63), youngest player, at 36, inducted into the Baseball Hall of Fame.

Sandy was born December 30, 1935, in Brooklyn, New York, to Jack and Evelyn Braun. His parents divorced while the future fastball and curveball king was still young, and he took the name of his stepfather.

Remarkably this pitching genius did not play baseball until his senior year in high school. His friends in Brooklyn were into basketball. Therefore, Sandy started his sports career playing on the basketball team.

When the future strikeout king finally did turn out for the baseball team, he played at first base.

Even at the University of Cincinnati playing basketball was more important to him. It was more important, also, to the university that had given him a basketball scholarship.

However, he did turn his attention to the mound. In 32 innings he struck out 51 batters, and had 18 K's in one game, 16 in another.

That freshman performance earned him more than a serious look from the major leagues. The New York Giants checked him out, but turned him down. The Brooklyn Dodgers (who had taken an interest in his high school sandlot games) gave him a trial. They, too decided he was not good enough. Neither, too, did Milwaukee nor Pittsburgh make an offer following a trial.

But the Dodgers relented, and on December 22, 1954, Koufax signed for a $14,000 bonus and a $6,000 salary.

He was now a professional baseball player on the strength of only 16 games and 100 pitched innings

Sandy Koufax prepares to hurl a strike (over) and smilingly sizes up his budding career (above).

in college.

Much was expected of him. As a bonus player he could not play in the minors—pitcher Tom La-Sorda, later manager of the Dodgers, was cut to make room for him—so it was a case of show and tell with the big boys.

He began telling early in his career. On August 27, 1955, pitching against the Cincinnati Reds, he fanned 14, and allowed only 2 hits on the way to his first of 165 career wins and his first of 40 shutouts.

In his next game, he showed his stuff when he pitched his second shutout. This time against the Pittsburgh Pirates, giving up 5 hits and fanning 6.

But he was a wild pitcher in those early years. He was used sparingly in his first season ('55), appearing in 12 games, winning 2 of 4 decisions, with 2 shutouts.

In his first 6 seasons, Sandy was an average pitcher, winning 36 and losing 40.

In those early years Koufax was learning how to pitch, developing the skills many sharpen in high school and hone in the minors. But while he was perhaps lacking in technique, he was showing the occasional excellent game that was a prelude to his undisputed brilliance.

On August 31, 1959, he struck out 18 San Francisco Giants to equal legendary Bob Feller's mark. When added to the 16 he had struck out the previous game against the Phillies, he had a 2-game strikeout record of 34—breaking another record.

Sandy is reported to have credited *Norm Sherry* (the brother of *Larry*) with advice that turned him from being an average to an outstanding pitcher.

Each year it appeared he was slowly establishing himself as a potential strikeout king of all time.

In 1961, he struck out 269—breaking Christy Mathewson's National League record of 267 set in 1903.

Yet he had not come close to his best years. These were to come in the next 5 years when the left-handed hurler was virtually invincible. But they were interrupted by a badly injured pitching finger in '62 and an arm injury in '64.

Each time he came back with brilliance. In '62 it was 14-7 and a league leading 2.54 ERA; in '63 it was 25 wins, 1.88 ERA, 306 strikeouts and 11 shutouts; in '65 it was 26 wins, 2.04 ERA and 382 strikeouts. Each time he re-established himself as the premier pitcher. Each time, however, took him closer to the unfortunate arthritis that was to cut short his brilliant baseball career.

In January 1972, 344 votes out of a possible 396 were cast in favor of Sandy Koufax entering the Baseball Hall of Fame.

18 Strikeouts #1

SAN FRANCISCO (N)	ab	r	h	rbi	LOS ANGELES (N)	ab	r	h	rbi
Brandt, 3b	4	0	0	0	Gilliam, 3b	4	2	1	0
Pagan, 3b	0	0	0	0	Moon, rf	4	2	1	3
McCovey, 1b	4	1	1	1	Larker, lf	2	0	0	0
Mays, cf	3	1	1	0	Snider, cf	3	0	1	1
Cepeda, lf	4	0	1	1	Hodges, 1b	3	0	1	0
Alou, rf	4	0	2	0	Neal, 2b	4	0	0	0
Schmidt, c	4	0	1	0	Roseboro, c	4	0	1	0
Bressoud, ss	4	0	0	0	Wills, ss	4	0	1	0
O'Connell, 2b	3	0	1	0	Koufax, p	3	1	1	0
Sanford, p	4	0	0	0		–	–	–	–
Worth'gton, p	0	0	0	0	Total	31	5	7	4
Total	34	2	7	2					

San Francisco	1	0	0	0	1	0	0	0	0—2
Los Angeles	1	0	0	0	0	0	0	1	3—5

One out when winning runs scored.
E—Brandt, Pagan, Cepeda. A—San Francisco 13, Los Angeles 4. LOB—San Francisco 7, Los Angeles 8.
2B Hits—Mays, Cepeda, O'Connell. HR—McCovey, Moon. 5B—Gilliam 2. Sacrifices—Koufax, Larker.

	IP	H	R	ER	BB	SO
Sanford (L, 12—11)	8⅓	6	4	4	5	7
Worthington	0	1	1	1	0	0
Koufax (W, 8—4)	9	7	2	2	2	18

(Worthington pitched to one batter in ninth.)
Wild pitches—Sanford 2. PB—Schmidt. Umpires—Gorman, Sudol, Boggess and Landes.
Time—2:54. Attendance—60,194.

18 Strikeouts #2

LOS ANGELES (N)	ab	r	h	rbi	CHICAGO (N)	ab	r	h	rbi
Willis, ss	4	1	0	0	Brock, cf	3	0	0	1
Gilliam, 2b,3b	4	1	1	0	Hubbs, 2b	4	0	0	0
Moon, 1b	4	3	3	0	Santo, 3b	4	0	2	0
Harkness, 1b	0	0	0	0	Banks, 1b	4	0	0	0
Snider, rf	3	2	2	3	Williams, lf	4	2	2	1
Fairly, rf	0	0	0	0	Will, rf	3	0	1	0
T. Davis, lf	5	2	2	4	White, ss	3	0	0	0
Roseboro, c	5	0	2	0	Thacker, c	3	0	1	0
W. Davis, cf	3	0	0	1	Cardwell, p	1	0	0	0
Carey, 3b	4	1	2	1	a)Rodgers	1	0	0	0
c)Burright, 2b	1	0	0	0	Balsamo, p	0	0	0	0
Koufax	4	0	0	0	b)McKnight	1	0	0	0
	–	–	–	–	Gerard, p	0	0	0	0
Total	37	10	12	9	Elston, p	0	0	0	0
					d)Morhardt	1	0	0	0
					Total	32	2	6	2

Los Angeles	0	2	1	1	3	0	1	0	2—10
Chicago	0	0	0	0	1	0	0	0	1— 2

E—Banks. A—Los Angeles 6, Chicago 12.
LOB—Los Angeles 7, Chicago 7.
2B Hits—Roseboro, Santo, Williams.
3B—Snider. HR—Carey, T. Davis, Snider, Williams. 5B—Wills, Moon, Burright. Sacrifice—Gilliam. 5F—W. Davis.

	IP	H	R	ER	BB	SO
Koufax (W, 3—1)	9	6	2	2	4	18
Caldwell (L, 0—4)	5	8	7	7	1	3
Balsamo	2	0	1	0	2	2
Gerard	1⅓	4	2	2	0	0
Elston	⅓	0	0	0	1	0

Wild pitch—Caldwell. Balk—Balsamo.
Umpires—Boggess, Landes, Smith, Steiner.
Time—2:41. Attendance—8,938.

ANSWERS

1. ▶ *Hank Greenberg.* On September 27, 1938, in the second game of a doubleheader at Briggs Stadium, the Detroit Tigers first baseman hit a home run in the third inning, his second of the game. Slick Coffman yielded 8 hits, as the Tigers defeated the St. Louis Browns, in a game halted by darkness after 7 innings, 10-2.

ALL-STARS

2. ▶ *Larry Sherry.* On October 2, 1959, in the eighth inning of the second game, Torgeson ran for Ted Kluszewski and scored on Al Smith's double. Johnny Podres, with relief help from Sherry, was the winning pitcher. The Los Angeles Dodgers defeated the Chicago White Sox, at Comiskey Park, 4-3. Bob Shaw took the loss. During the Series, pitching in relief, Sherry hurled 12⅔ innings, won 2 games and had 2 saves.

1960-
PRESENT

3. ▶ *Ron Blomberg.* On April 6, 1973, in the first inning on Opening Day, Luis Tiant walked Blomberg with the bases loaded scoring Matty Alou. Tiant and the Boston Red Sox defeated the New York Yankees, at Fenway Park, 15-5.

1930-59

4. ▶ Babe Ruth. On September 29, 1934, in the seventh inning, Ruth hit a 3-run homer. Cohen yielded 11 hits, as the Washington Senators defeated the New York Yankees, at Griffith Stadium, 8-5. John Broaca was the losing pitcher.

OLD-TIMERS
1857-1929

5. ▶ *Ed Reulbach.* On June 30, 1909, Reulbach and the Chicago Cubs defeated the Pittsburgh Pirates, 3-2. Vic Willis, who won 248 games in his 13-year career, took the loss. Forbes Field was the home of the Pirates from 1909 to 1970.

BASEBALL
MISCELLANY

6. ▶ *Al Schacht.* In 1921 he teamed up with another Washington coach, Nick Altrock, for a combination burlesque prize fight, pantomime tightwire walk, and stint as a band leader before the World Series.

HALL
OF
FAME
7. ► Nicknamed "Stan the Man," this Cardinals Hall of Famer hit the first home run allowed by *Sandy Koufax* . . . ?

ALL-STARS
8. ► Which hurler, known as "Rapid Robert," surrendered *Harry Danning's* only All-Star Game hit?

1960-
PRESENT
9. ► In which Chicago stadium, in 1969, did *Mike Epstein* hit 3 home runs in 1 game?

1930-59
10. ► *Joe Ginsberg* caught this pitcher's first no-hitter of the 1952 season . . . ?

OLD-TIMERS
1857-1929
11. ► Which Phillies Jewish pitcher surrendered Honus Wagner's 3,000th career hit?

BASEBALL
MISCELLANY
12. ► In 1866, this Jewish second baseman became baseball's first professional player . . . ?

(Answers next page.)

ANSWERS

HALL OF FAME

7. ▶ Stan Musial. On September 15, 1955, in the third inning, Musial and Rip Repulski hit consecutive home runs. Koufax was removed from the game after 4 innings. Alex Grammas' twelfth-inning single scored Repulski with the winning run. The St. Louis Cardinals defeated the Brooklyn Dodgers, at Busch Stadium, 3-2.

ALL-STARS

8. ▶ Bob Feller. On July 9, 1940, in the eighth inning, Mel Ott walked, was sacrificed to second, and scored on Danning's single. The National League defeated the American League, at Sportsman's Park, 4-0.

1960-PRESENT

9. ▶ Comiskey Park. On May 16, 1969, the Washington Senators' first baseman hit home runs in the first and sixth innings off Sammy Ellis. In the seventh inning, Epstein hit his eighth home run of the season off relief pitcher Wilbur Wood. Despite this batting display, the Chicago White Sox defeated the Senators, 7-6. Epstein hit 30 homers for the season.

1930-59

10. ▶ Virgil Trucks. On May 15, 1952, in the ninth inning, Vic Wertz' 2-out home run ended the game. Trucks and the Detroit Tigers defeated the Washington Senators, at Briggs Stadium, 1-0. Bob Porterfield, who allowed 4 hits, took the loss.

OLD-TIMERS 1857-1928

11. ▶ *Erskine Mayer.* On June 9, 1914, Wagner led off the ninth inning with a double and later scored on a ground out. Mayer yielded 5 hits, as the Philadelphia Phillies defeated the Pittsburgh Pirates, at Baker Bowl, 3-1. Joe Conzelman was the losing pitcher.

BASEBALL MISCELLANY

12. ▶ *Lipman Pike.* He played for 5 teams in a short major league career—1876-78, 81 and 87 yet batted .304 in 163 games.

13. ▶ This Cardinals Hall of Famer, elected to the Cooperstown Hall in 1970, was pitching when *Hank Greenberg* stole home in a World Series game . . . ?

14. ▶ This Indians Jewish slugger had the only hit allowed by Hoyt Wilhelm in a World Series game . . . ?

15. ▶ Bob Rodgers caught which Angels 1962 no-hitter?

16. ▶ This Giants Jewish batter was the only player ever to pinch-hit for Hall of Famer Mel Ott . . . ?

17. ▶ Ty Cobb was removed for a pinch-hitter for the first time in his career when opposing this St. Louis Browns Jewish hurler . . . ?

18. ▶ This non-Jewish Hall of Famer is buried in a Baltimore Jewish Cemetery . . . ?

(Answers on page 18.)

JEWISH BASEBALL NEWS   **Bulletin**

GREENBERG TRADES RIFLE FOR BAT

In 1941 the clouds of war swirled about the world.

In the United States, men and women hurried off to do war work and members of the military were shipped off to join fighting forces in foreign lands.

At that time, *Henry Greenberg* was playing baseball as the highest paid player in the American League.

For 10 years, wearing the uniform of the Detroit Tigers, he had dazzled the public with his exploits at the plate.

That year, however, he put down his bat and picked up a rifle when drafted into the U.S. Army.

Within six months, he was a sergeant. At that time, because he was near the age limit for service in the military, he was released.

December 7, 1941, was the infamous date of the invasion of Pearl Harbor.

'Hank' Greenberg immediately volunteered for military service.

Promoted into the officer ranks, he was assigned to the China-Burma-India war theater where he ran the Headquarters squadron of the 20th Bomber Command.

For the next three years, the one-time $60,000-a-year first baseman and home-run king was involved in the day-to-day work of seeing to the safety of Allied servicemen fighting in World War II.

With the end of the war, 'Hank' Greenberg returned to active duty for the Tigers.

* * * *

It is the last day of the '45 American League's regular season. Detroit faces the St. Louis Browns at Sportsman's Park in a game they have to win in order to face the Chicago Cubs in the World Series.

The top of the ninth inning. Bases loaded.

Greenberg's 6-4 frame hulks at the plate. Nels Potter, the Browns' top hurler winds up. The pitch... ...Greenberg connects.

The shot that used to sting across the Burma Pass now heads toward left field, 351 feet away. Home run.

The Tigers win the pennant.

They win the World Series in 7 games ('Hank' belted 2 of the only 3 homers in the Series). And 'Hank' is back in baseball.

* * * *

truly yours
Hank Greenberg

Hank Greenberg was born on January 1, 1911, in New York City. His parents emigrated from Rumania and later settled in the Bronx, where Hank played baseball and basketball at James Monroe High School. After rejecting several offers, he signed a professional baseball contract with the Detroit Tigers that enabled him to attend college (New York University). He yearned for a baseball career and was assigned to Hartford, Connecticut, in the Eastern League in 1930. In view of his poor start (.214 average in 17 games), he was sent to Raleigh, North Carolina in the Piedmont League, where he batted .314 and had 19 home runs and 93 RBI. At the end of the year, Hank was recalled by the Tigers and appeared in one game as a pinch-hitter.

In 1931, he was the first baseman for Evansville, Indiana, in the Three-I League (15 home runs and a .318 average), and the following season with Beaumont was the Texas League's Most Valuable Player (39 home runs, 131 RBI and a .290 average).

Hank joined the Tigers in 1933 and batted .301, before having a sparkling season (26 home runs, 139 RBI and a .339 average) for the 1934 pennant-winners. The following year, he was selected the league's MVP (36 home runs, 170 RBI and a .328 average). Injuries limited his participation in the World Series, and also curtailed his playing time to 12 games in 1936. He returned the next year in an explosive manner, banging out 40 home runs, with a league-leading 183 RBI and a .337 average. Also, he collected 200 hits for the third time in his career.

In 1938, Hank belted 58 home runs. Eleven times during the season he hit 2 home runs in one game, including 4 in succession. Following another year with the Tigers (33 home runs, 112 RBI and a .312 average), he was moved to the outfield to make room for Rudy York at first base. Hank responded with another MVP trophy for the 1940 pennant-winners; he led the league in home runs (41) and RBI (150), and had a .340 average.

He returned from World War II and helped the Tigers to the pennant with a grand slam homer on the final day of the season. In

Grand Slam Wins Pennant

DETROIT (A)	ab	r	h	e	ST. LOUIS (A)	ab	r	h	e
Webb, ss	3	1	1	0	Gutte'go, 2b	3	1	1	0
Mayo, 2b	4	0	1	0	Finney, lf	2	0	2	0
Cramer, cf	5	1	1	0	Bryant, rf	2	0	0	0
Greenb'g, lf	5	1	2	0	c)Christnian	1	0	0	0
Cullen'e, rf	4	1	1	0	Gray, c	1	1	0	0
York, 1b	5	0	0	0	McQuinn, 1b	4	0	1	0
Outlaw, 3b	3	0	1	0	Moore, rf	4	1	1	0
Richards, c	4	0	1	0	Stephens, ss	4	0	2	0
Trucks, p	1	0	1	0	Mancuso,c	4	0	0	5
Newhou'r, p	0	0	0	0	Schults, 3b	4	0	0	0
a)Walker	1	0	1	0	Potter, p	3	0	1	0
b)Boron	0	1	0	0		—	—	—	—
Benton, p	0	0	0	0	Total	32	3	8	0
	—	—	—	—					
Total	35	6	9	0					

a(Batted for Newhouser in ninth; b) Ran for Walker in ninth; c) Batted for Byrnes in sixth.

| Detroit | 0 | 0 | 0 | 0 | 1 | 1 | 0 | 0 | 4—4 |
| St. Louis | 1 | 0 | 0 | 0 | 0 | 0 | 1 | 1 | 0—3 |

Runs batted in—Finney, Mayo, Richards, Stephens, McQuinn, Greenberg (4). Two-base hits—Gutteridge, Potter, McQuinn, Moore. Home run—Greenberg. Sacrifice hits—Webb, Mayo. Double plays—Richards and Mayo; Outlaw; Mayo and York. Left on bases—St. Louis 5, Detroit 0, Bases on balls—Off Trucks 2, Potter 5, Neuhauser 1. Struck out—By Trucks 3, Potter 4, Neuhauser 3. Hits—Off Trucks 3 in 5½ innings. Newhauser 1 in 2⅔. Benton 1 in 1. Winning pitcher —Neuhauser. Umpires—Pipgras, Berry, Rue and Hubbard. Time of game—2:23. Attendance—5,582.

1946, he again led the league in home runs (44) and RBI (127). In a controversial move that had the

16

Cincinnati Reds World Champions 1940

(Top Row) Turner, Ripple, Vander Meer, M. McCormick, Shoffner, Guise, Craft, Frey, Beggs; (Middle Row) Traveling Secretary *Paul*, Moore, Joost, Lombardi, Walters, F. McCormick, Derringer, Hutchings, Baker, General Manager Giles; (Bottom Row) Riggs, Goodman, Thompson, *Arnovich*, Coach Gowdy, Manager McKechnie, Coach Wilson, Werber, Myers, Riddle, Trainer Rohde.

baseball world buzzing for more than a season, he was sold to the Pittsburgh Pirates and belted 25 homers in his final year.

Greenberg's statistics: 1,394 games, 1,628 hits in 5,193 at-bats, 1,051 runs scored, including 331 home runs, 1,276 RBI, a .313 career batting average and a .605 slugging percentage. He appeared in 4 World Series, with 27 hits, including 5 home runs, 22 RBI and a .318 average.

Hank led the league in home runs and RBI 4 times, had 11 career grand slam home runs, led the league twice in doubles, and was selected to the All-Star Team 4 times, and twice was the league's MVP.

He was admitted to the Baseball Hall of Fame (1956), and the Jewish Sports Hall of Fame in Netanya, Israel (1979).

'Hank' Greenberg was a hero in both fields.

ANSWERS

13. ► Jessie Haines. On October 6, 1934, in the eighth inning of the fourth game, Haines relieved Bill Walker. Marv Owen's single scored 1 run and sent *Greenberg,* who had doubled, to third. As the St. Louis Cardinals pitcher struck out Pete Fox, the runners completed a double steal. Second baseman Frank Frisch's return throw to the plate got away from the catcher Bill DeLancey. *Greenberg* raced home for a "stolen" run and Owen advanced to third base. Eldon Auker was the winning pitcher, as the Detroit Tigers defeated the Cardinals, at Sportsman's Park, 10-4.

14. ► *Al Rosen.* On October 2, 1954, in the eighth inning of the fourth and final game, *Rosen* singled off the New York Giants relief pitcher. The Giants defeated the Cleveland Indians, at Municipal Stadium, 7-4.

15. ► *Bo Belinsky.* On May 5, 1962, *Belinsky* hurled a no-hitter and had 9 strikeouts, 4 walks and 2 hit batsmen. The Los Angeles Angels defeated the Baltimore Orioles, at Chavez Ravine, 2-0.

16. ► *Sid Gordon.* On September 2, 1946, in the seventh inning of the second game of a doubleheader, *Gordon* hit a run-scoring pinch-hit single. The New York Giants, with 8 runs in the seventh inning, defeated the Boston Braves, at Braves Field, 8-3. Hal Schumacher was the winning pitcher.

17. ► *Barney Pelty.* On April 24, 1906, in the ninth inning, Sam Crawford batted for Cobb and singled. *Pelty* yielded 4 hits, as the St. Louis Browns defeated the Detroit Tigers, at Sportsman's Park, 2-0.

18. ► Rube Marquard. This New York Giants hurler had a 19-game winning streak in 1912.

HALL
OF
FAME

19. ▶ This Hall of Famer caught *Sandy Koufax'* first major league shutout...?

ALL-STARS

20. ▶ Dave McNally surrendered the first career hit to this Twins player who later won several batting titles...?

1960-
PRESENT

21. ▶ In a 1960 game, *Larry Sherry* was the winning pitcher when this relative hit a home run...?

1930-59

22. ▶ This Yankees pitcher, nicknamed "Steady Eddie," yielded *Saul Rogovin*'s first major league home run...?

OLD-TIMERS
1857-1929

23. ▶ This early twentieth century Cubs Jewish hurler led the National League in pitching percentage for 3 consecutive years (1906-08)...?

BASEBALL
MISCELLANY

24. ▶ Which Jewish native of Alabama became "The Voice of the Yankees"?

         (Answers next page.)

ANSWERS

19. ▶ Roy Campanella. On August 27, 1955, the Brooklyn Dodgers rookie surrendered a first-inning single to Ted Kluszewski and a ninth-inning double to Sam Mele. *Koufax* had 14 strikeouts, as the Dodgers defeated the Cincinnati Reds, at Ebbets Field, 7-0. Art Fowler was the losing pitcher. Campanella's career was cut short by a car accident which left him paralyzed.

20. ▶ *Rod Carew.* On April 11, 1967, the Twins second baseman debuted on Opening Day with 2 hits. Moe Drabowsky was the winning pitcher, as the Baltimore Orioles defeated the Minnesota Twins, at Memorial Stadium, 6-3. Jim Kaat took the loss.

21. ▶ *Norm Sherry* (brother). On May 7, 1960, in the eleventh inning, catcher *Norm Sherry* homered off Ruben Gomez. Sherry's brother, *Larry,* hurled 4 innings and allowed 2 hits and 1 run in relief, as the Los Angeles Dodgers defeated the Philadelphia Phillies, at Los Angeles Memorial Coliseum, 3-2. This was the first game in which *Larry* and *Norm Sherry* appeared together as a battery.

22. ▶ Ed Lopat. On July 23, 1950, in the second inning, the Detroit Tigers pitcher hit a grand slam homer which scored Hoot Evers, Don Kollaway and Bob Swift. *Rogovin* left the game in the sixth inning. The Tigers scored 2 runs in the ninth inning to defeat the New York Yankees, at Yankee Stadium, 6-5. *Rogovin* won the American League ERA Title in 1951.

23. ▶ *Ed Reulbach* with season records of 20-4, 17-4 and 24-7.

24. ▶ *Mel Allen.*

25. ▶ This Cardinals Hall of Famer surrendered a home run to *Hank Greenberg*, who was appearing in his first World Series game...?

26. ▶ Bill Heath and Gene Oliver combined to catch which Jewish hurler's first no-hitter?

27. ▶ This Red Sox reliever, nicknamed "The Monster," was the losing pitcher in *Alan Koch*'s first major league victory...?

28. ▶ *Don Taussig* hit his first home run in this San Francisco stadium...?

29. ▶ Clarence Mitchell surrendered this Jewish scholar's first career hit...?

30. ▶ Hall of Famer Joe DiMaggio was married to this Hollywood actress, who converted to Judaism...?

(Answers next page.)

ANSWERS

25. ▶ Dizzy Dean. On October 3, 1934, in the eighth inning of the first game, Greenberg homered. Dean yielded 8 hits, as the St. Louis Cardinals defeated the Detroit Tigers, at Navin Field, 8-3.

26. ▶ *Ken Holtzman.* On August 19, 1969, Heath and Oliver were behind the plate during *Holtzman's* historic game. In this pitching duel Ron Santo hit a 3-run homer in the first inning. *Holtzman* and the Chicago Cubs defeated the Atlanta Braves, at Wrigley Field, 3-0.

27. ▶ Dick Radatz. On August 8, 1963, Koch entered the game in the tenth inning and allowed 1 hit. The Detroit Tigers, with 1 run in the tenth inning, defeated the Boston Red Sox, at Tiger Stadium, 6-5.

28. ▶ Seals Stadium. On June 6, 1958, the San Francisco Giants rightfielder led off the third inning with a homer off Harvey Haddix. The Cincinnati Reds defeated the Giants, 5-4.

29. ▶ *Moe Berg.* On June 27, 1923, in the seventh inning, *Berg* debuted as the Brooklyn Robins shortstop. In the eighth inning, he singled and later scored on Jimmy Johnston's triple. Dutch Ruether yielded 11 hits, as the Robins defeated the Philadelphia Phillies, at Baker Bowl, 15-5. Lefty Weinert was the losing pitcher.

30. ▶ *Marilyn Monroe*, the internationally-acclaimed actress and star of "Gentlemen Prefer Blondes."

HALL
OF
FAME

31. ▶ This Braves Hall of Famer surrendered *Sandy Koufax'* first career home run...?

ALL-STARS

32. ▶ In 1953, Dick Marlowe surrendered this Indians Jewish slugger's league-leading 43rd home run...?

1960-
PRESENT

33. ▶ In 1962, which Jewish player caught the expansion New York Mets first game at the Polo Grounds?

1930-59

34. ▶ In 1938, Jewish players *Morrie Arnovich* and *Phil Weintraub* were the first pinch-hitters in a regularly scheduled National League game at this stadium...?

OLD-TIMERS
1857-1929

35. ▶ In a 1906 World Series Game, Jiggs Donahue belted the only hit off this Cubs Jewish pitcher...?

BASEBALL
MISCELLANY

36. ▶ Which noted first baseman was nicknamed "Super Jew"?

ANSWERS

HALL
OF
FAME

31. ► Warren Spahn. On June 13, 1962, *Koufax'* fifth-inning homer gave the Los Angeles Dodgers a 2-run lead. *Koufax* yielded 3 hits, as the Dodgers defeated the Milwaukee Braves, at County Stadium, 2-1.

ALL-STARS

32. ► *Al Rosen.* On September 25, 1953, in the eighth inning, *Rosen* hit his second home run of the game. Dick Tomanek debuted and yielded 6 hits, as the Cleveland Indians defeated the Detroit Tigers, 12-3. *Rosen* led the league in home runs and runs-batted-in. His .336 average was only .001 behind the leader.

1960-
PRESENT

33. ► *Joe Ginsberg.* On April 13, 1962, in their home opener, the New York Mets used pitchers Sherman Jones, Herb Moford and Ray Daviault. Tom Sturdivant was the winning pitcher, as the Pittsburgh Pirates defeated the Mets, 4-3. Frank Thomas homered for the Mets.

1930-59

34. ► Shibe Park, Philadelphia. On July 4, 1938, in the first game of a doubleheader, Boston Bees pitcher Bobby Reis retired both pinch-hitters. The Bees defeated the Philadelphia Phillies, 10-5. The Phillies moved from Baker Bowl to share Shibe Park with the Athletics. The Phillies played at Shibe Park, later renamed Connie Mack Stadium, from 1938-70.

OLD-TIMERS
1857-1929

35. ► *Ed Reulbach.* On October 10, 1906, in the seventh inning of the second game, Donahue singled. The Chicago Cubs defeated the Chicago White Sox, at South Side Park, 7-1.

BASEBALL
MISCELLANY

36. ► *Mike Epstein.* In a 9-year career he played for Baltimore, Washington, Oakland, Texas and California, and slugged 130 home runs.

HALL
OF
FAME

37. ► In a 1923 game, *Samuel Bohne*'s single was the only hit off this Hall of Famer, nicknamed "Dazzy"...?

ALL-STARS

38. ► In a 1949 game, Ken Raffensberger and Johnny Vander Meer each surrendered a home run in one inning to this Giants Jewish batter...?

1960-
PRESENT

39. ► *Steve Stone*, the 1980 American League Cy Young Award winner, hurled his first career win in this Pittsburgh stadium...?

1930-59

40. ► *Harry Eisenstat* was the winning pitcher when this Indians Hall of Famer fanned 18 batters in one game...?

OLD-TIMERS
1857-1929

41. ► This Jewish catcher led the National League in putouts for 6 consecutive years (1902-1907)...?

BASEBALL
MISCELLANY

42. ► Nicknamed "Dolly," this Jewish umpire was a holdout in 1936...?

 (Answers on page 28.)

JEWISH BASEBALL NEWS   Final

GIANTS' JEWISH SECOND BASEMAN

It's tough to fill the shoes of a Hall of Famer. It's tougher still to be labeled the Great Jewish Hope.

But this was the challenge *Andy Cohen* accepted when he replaced Rogers Hornsby at second base with the New York Giants in 1928.

He began the season successfully, scattering hits right and left.

But the media hype added to the pressure of the pitchers on the mound and Andy tailed off, ending the season with a .274 average.

The next year, he fit into those Hall of Fame shoes excellently and showed power at the plate, but the boys in the front office were not satisfied with a .294 average.

Feeling let down, they shipped Andy Cohen off to the minors where he etched out a more than respectable 10-year career.

The oldest of three children to Manus, a native of Lithuania, and Lena Cohen, from Kiev, Russia, was born October 25, 1904, in Baltimore, Maryland. Andy's family moved to El Paso, Texas, when he was age four.

Making a name for himself became more than a hobby as he excelled in baseball, football and basketball through elementary school and El Paso High School, before graduating in 1922.

"That year I signed a contract with Galveston in the Texas

League, but I saw my future in the business world so accepted a scholarship to the University of Alabama."

He quit college in his senior year.

"I wanted to go into pro baseball. I had decided that was my goal."

(His younger brother, Sydney, followed in his footsteps, and later became a pitcher for the Washington Senators.)

In the 3 years since signing his contract, Galveston had been bought by Waco, for whom Andy batted .312 in '25.

On the strength of his abilities at the plate—and the goals of the front office marketing boys who had analyzed the potential baseball customers in New York and saw lots of Jewish fans who needed a reason to go through the turnstiles—he was purchased by the New York Giants for $25,000.

This was the same amount of money Waco had earlier shelled out to purchase the entire Galveston franchise!

His attempt to be a Great Jewish Baseball Player began as a pinch hitter for Hall of Famer Frankie Frisch. He singled off Ray Pierce at Philadelphia's Baker Bowl in 1926.

"Manager John McGraw had a great sense of humor," Andy re-

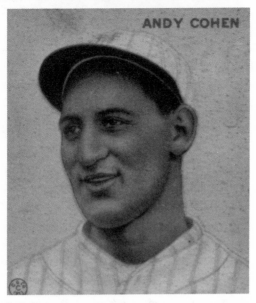

Only 5-8, 155 pounds, Andy Cohen batted .312 with Waco Cubs (1925) before he was signed to play for the New York Giants.

calls. "A few moments later he said, 'Young man, congratulations! Today you are leading the National League in hitting.'"

For the remainder of that season, he stayed with the Giants as a reserve infielder.

Those watchful boys in the front office kept their eyes on Andy through his next year during which he batted .353 with Buffalo, the International League pennant-winners. On the strength of his work at the plate and in the field, he was named to the All-Star team at shortstop.

Then came his big moment as the Great Jewish Hope.

When the dream evaporated, he returned to play in the minors where he had an excellent career through Newark (International League) in '30-31 and Minneapolis (American Association) in '32-40.

"I knew that when I quit college in my senior year for baseball, that baseball would be my life," he said.

If he couldn't make it as a player, he knew he would make it as a coach.

After a 2-year stint as a player/manager and military service, he became a Boston Braves scout in '45, and began managing minor league teams. He also had a 1-year stint as a coach—and a 1-day assignment as a manager—of the Philadelphia Phillies.

But Andy Cohen's love for his adopted home of Texas kept tugging at him. He eventually found the ideal locale for his twin loves with the University of Texas at El Paso where for 17 years he was their highly-successful baseball coach.

Here he found life more rewarding than being New York's Great Jewish hope.

27

ANSWERS

HALL
OF
FAME

37. ▶ Dazzy Vance. On June 17, 1923, with 2 out in the ninth inning, this Cincinnati Reds second baseman singled to center field. The Brooklyn Robins defeated the Reds, at Redland Field, 9-0. Pete Donahue was the losing pitcher.

ALL-STARS

38. ▶ *Sid Gordon.* On July 31, 1949, in the second inning of the second game of a doubleheader, the New York Giants scored 9 runs highlighted by *Gordon's* homers. His second home run, with 2 men on, was his twenty-third of the season. Adrian Zabala yielded 5 hits, as the Giants blanked the Cincinnati Reds, at Crosley Field, 9-0.

1960-
PRESENT

39. ▶ Three Rivers Stadium. On April 23, 1971, *Stone* yielded 5 hits when notching his first major league victory. The San Francisco Giants defeated the Pittsburgh Pirates, 2-0. Luke Walker took the loss.

1930-59

40. ▶ Bob Feller. On October 2, 1938, in the first game of a doubleheader, *Eisenstat* yielded 4 hits in winning his ninth game against 6 defeats. The Detroit Tigers defeated the Cleveland Indians, at Municipal Stadium, 4-1.

OLD-TIMERS
1857-1929

41. ▶ *Johnny Kling.*

BASEBALL
MISCELLANY

42. ▶ *Dolly Stark.* He also is credited with many innovations in baseball umpiring.

43. ▶ *Art Shamsky*'s first major league home run came as a pinch-hitter for this Reds Hall of Famer...?

44. ▶ *Conrad Cardinal* debuted in relief of this Houston pitcher, who later lost a no-hitter...?

45. ▶ In 1965, Claude Osteen surrendered this Jewish Astros' first career hit...?

46. ▶ In 1959, Joe Pignatano caught this Dodgers Jewish pitcher's only major league shutout...?

47. ▶ This Jewish pitcher was the winning hurler in the first game ever played at White Sox (Comiskey) Park...?

48. ▶ This Jewish outfielder was known as "The Rabbi of Swat"...?

(Answers next page.)

ANSWERS

43. ► Frank Robinson. On May 2, 1965, in the fifth inning of the first game of a doubleheader, the Cincinnati Reds scored 8 runs highlighted by *Shamsky*'s 2-run homer off Tom Parsons. Jim Maloney yielded 8 hits, as the Reds defeated the New York Mets, at Crosley Field, 9-4. Robinson was removed in the fourth inning due to an injury.

44. ► Ken Johnson. On April 11, 1963, Cardinal relieved Johnson and yielded 1 run and 3 hits in 3 innings. Billy O'Dell and the San Francisco Giants defeated the Houston Colt .45s, at Colt Stadium, 7-1. Johnson subsequently lost a no-hitter 1-0, to Cincinnati on April 23, 1964.

45. ► *Norm Miller.* On September 11, 1965, Miller debuted and had a pinch-hit single. However, it was not enough for a win as Osteen and the Los Angeles Dodgers defeated the Houston Astros, at Dodger Stadium, 8-3.

46. ► *Larry Sherry.* On September 11, 1959, in the second game of a doubleheader, *Sherry* yielded 6 hits and had 11 strikeouts. The Los Angeles Dodgers defeated the Pittsburgh Pirates, at the Los Angeles Memorial Coliseum, 4-0. Fred Green took the loss.

47. ► *Barney Pelty.* On July 1, 1910, *Pelty* yielded 5 hits, as the St. Louis Browns defeated the Chicago White Sox, 2-0. Ed Walsh was the losing pitcher.

48. ► *Moe Solomon.* In his only major league season, 1923, this outfielder had 1 RBI in 2 games and a .375 average.

HALL
OF
FAME

49. ► *Hank Greenberg* hit 306 home runs with the Detroit Tigers. He hit his first National League homer in this Chicago stadium...?

ALL-STARS

50. ► This Indians Jewish player holds the American League record for most home runs by a rookie in one season...?

1960-
PRESENT

51. ► *Art Shamsky*'s only career grand slam home run led to a victory for this Mets hurler, nicknamed "Tom Terrific"...?

1930-59

52. ► In a 1944 game, the New York Giants scored 26 runs, a club record for most runs in a game since 1900. Which Jewish pitcher gained the victory?

OLD-TIMERS
1857-1929

53. ► This nineteenth-century lefthanded catcher caught *William Kling*'s first major league victory...?

BASEBALL
MISCELLANY

54. ► Who was the Jewish businessman who owned the 1882 Cincinnati Reds, the first American Association pennant winner?

      (Answers next page.)

ANSWERS

49. ▶ Wrigley Field. On April 17, 1947, the Pittsburgh Pirates first baseman homered in the second inning off Hank Wyse. The Pirates defeated the Chicago Cubs, 7-1. Preacher Roe was the winning pitcher. *Greenberg* hit 25 home runs in his last season in the major leagues.

50. ▶ *Al Rosen* hit 37 home runs in 1950.

51. ▶ Tom Seaver. On August 30, 1968, *Shamsky*'s home run off Nelson Briles highlighted the Mets' 6-run fifth inning. Orlando Cepeda's double leading off the eighth inning was the St. Louis Cardinals' first hit. Seaver yielded 3 hits, as the New York Mets defeated the Cardinals, at Shea Stadium, 8-2.

52. ▶ *Harry Feldman.* On April 30, 1944, in the first game of a doubleheader, *Feldman* relieved Cliff Melton and allowed 1 run in 5⅔ innings. The New York Giants defeated the Brooklyn Dodgers, at the Polo Grounds, 26-8.

53. ▶ Jack Clements. On August 13, 1891, *Kling* yielded 10 hits, as the Philadelphia Phillies defeated the Pittsburgh Pirates, at Philadelphia Ball Park, 7-6. Mark Baldwin took the loss.

54. ▶ *Aaron Stern.* The American Association was a rival to the National League. Out of this short-lived league came the percentage system to determine the winner at the end of the season—the system used today.

HALL
OF
FAME
55. ► This Jewish pitcher won the first Los Angeles victory at Dodgers Stadium...?

ALL-STARS
56. ► This Tigers 30-game winner surrendered *Mike Epstein's* fourth consecutive home run during the 1971 season...?

1960-
PRESENT
57. ► In 1981, John Lowenstein's 2 home runs enabled this Jewish Cy Young Award hurler to win his 107th and last major league victory...?

1930-59
58. ► In a 1924 game, Jim Bottomley had 12 runs batted in and set a major league record. Twenty years later, this Jewish player for the Giants approached the record with 11 RBI...?

OLD-TIMERS
1857-1929
59. ► Which Jewish outfielder, in only his second full season, won the American League batting title in 1906?

BASEBALL
MISCELLANY
60. ► Nicknamed "Lefty," he managed the California Angels (1969-1971)...?

(Answers next page.)

ANSWERS

55. ► *Sandy Koufax.* On April 11, 1962, Koufax yielded 4 hits as the Los Angeles Dodgers defeated the Cincinnati Reds, 6-2. Jim Gilliam hit a 2-run homer. Moe Drabowsky took the loss. On April 10th, the Dodgers lost their home opener to the Reds, 6-3.

56. ► Denny McLain. On June 16, 1971, the Oakland Athletics first baseman belted solo home runs in the first and third innings. Vida Blue yielded 6 hits, on his way to his fourteenth win against two defeats. The Athletics defeated the Washington Senators, at the Oakland Coliseum, 5-1. The previous day, Epstein had homered off Jim Shellenback and Denny Riddleberger.

57. ► *Steve Stone.* On September 5, 1981, in the sixth inning, Terry Crowley and Lowenstein hit consecutive home runs. Lowenstein also hit a solo homer in the eighth inning. *Stone* allowed 6 hits in 7 innings and was relieved by Tippy Martinez. The Baltimore Orioles defeated the Oakland Athletics, at Memorial Stadium, 5-3. Rick Langford was the losing pitcher.

58. ► *Phil Weintraub.* On April 30, 1944, in the eighth inning of the first game of a doubleheader, *Weintraub's* 3-run homer off Tommy Warren highlighted his batting feat. The first baseman also had 2 doubles and a triple, as the New York Giants defeated the Brooklyn Dodgers, 26-8. Catcher Ernie Lombardi had seven runs batted in.

59. ► *George Stone.* That year he had a .358 average. In a 7-year career he closed out with a .301 average.

60. ► *Harold Phillips.*

HALL
OF
FAME

61. ▶ This Jewish slugger holds the Detroit Tigers all-time record for the most doubles in one season...?

ALL-STARS

62. ▶ In a 1940 game, Joe Bowman surrendered the home run which enabled this Giants Jewish slugger to hit for the cycle...?

1960-
PRESENT

63. ▶ *Ron Blomberg* made his major league debut in this Washington stadium...?

1930-59

64. ▶ This Cincinnati Reds pitcher, known as "Milkman Jim," surrendered *Sid Gordon*'s first major league hit...?

OLD-TIMERS
1857-1929

65. ▶ *Ike Danning* had 3 hits and a .500 career batting average. This Hall of Fame pitcher, known as "Red," allowed his first hit...?

BASEBALL
MISCELLANY

66. ▶ Who was the Jewish catcher who knew a dozen languages?

       (Answers on page 38.)

GINSBERG HANDS OVER TRAVEL TICKET

A veteran catcher, *Joe Ginsberg* played for 7 teams in 13 years.

"I was like a tour guide," he said recently from Detroit where he lives with his second wife, Donna.

He was signed to his first professional contract by Wish Egan, the Detroit Tigers head scout. That was in 1944 while he was in the twelfth grade at Cooley High School in Detroit.

"They sent me to Jamestown, New York, in the Pony League where I batted .270."

A stint in the U.S. Army interrupted the professional career of the son of Joseph, who emigrated from Galicia, and Rose, who emigrated from Austria. But time in the military didn't interrupt his work as an outfielder, third baseman and catcher.

"I was assigned to special services in the Philippines. There I played baseball with Early Wynn and Joe Garagiola."

After his time in uniform, in '47, the Tigers shipped him off to Williamsport, Pennsylvania, in the Eastern League. He just missed winning the batting title the next season, finishing with a .326 average.

At the end of '48, he was promoted to the majors. His first game was at Briggs Stadium, where he caught Lou Kretlow, had 1 hit and scored the winning run.

Although in 11 games, with 13

After a 13-year catching career, *Joe Ginsberg* hands over travel ticket and dons a business suit.

hits and a .361 average, the next year he played for Toledo, Ohio, in the American Association.

He returned to the Tigers in 1950, appearing in over 100 games in 1951 and 1952.

In '52 he caught 1 of 2 no-hitters hurled by Virgil Trucks, and had the only hit to spoil a Vic Raschi no-hitter.

"I hit a home run off Vic at Yankee Stadium in the eighth inning," he recalls. "They beat us 11-1."

He was traded to the Cleveland Indians in 1953, in a deal that involved eight players (Joe, Art

Other legendary catchers, *Ike Danning*, St. Louis (A), record-setter *Johnny Kling*, Chicago Cubs, Boston (N), Cincinnati, and *Mike Simon*, Pittsburgh, St. Louis (F), Brooklyn (F).

Houtteman, Owen Friend and Bill Wight for Ray Boone, Al Aber, Steve Gromek and Dick Weik).

He played several games for the 1954 World Series-bound Indians.

The next season the touring career of Joe Ginsberg stopped at the minors again. This time with Seattle, for whom he played through the '55 Pacific Coast League championship.

Then it was off to the Kansas City Athletics, in a deal that involved Lou Kretlow and $100,000.

The next year he put on the Baltimore Orioles uniform as their reserve catcher (1956-60).

He then played for the Chicago White Sox and the Boston Red Sox.

The last stop in his major league career came when he opened the '62 season with the expansion New York Mets.

"I got a call from the general manager. I caught that first day at the Polo Grounds."

Joe Ginsberg finished out the year as a player/coach with Denver in the American Association.

Before he finished his career as a professional baseball player, Joe had appeared in 695 major league games, collecting 414 hits, with a .241 batting average.

Then he turned in his much-used travel ticket.

ANSWERS

61. ▶ *Hank Greenberg.* In 1934 he hit 63 doubles.

62. ▶ *Harry Danning.* On June 15, 1940, in the fifth inning, *Danning* hit a 3-run inside-the-park home run. He followed this blast with a triple in the sixth inning off Johnny Lanning. Hal Schumacher was the winning pitcher, as the New York Giants defeated the Pittsburgh Pirates, at the Polo Grounds, 12-1.

63. ▶ Robert F. Kennedy Memorial Stadium. On September 10, 1969, in the eighth inning, Jimmy Hall doubled and scored on Jerry Kenney's single. *Blomberg* pinch-hit for New York Yankees hurler Bill Burbach and walked. Dick Bosman yielded 2 hits, as the Washington Senators defeated the Yankees, 6-1. Mel Stottlemyre was the losing pitcher. Frank Howard and Ken McMullen hit home runs.

64. ▶ Jim Turner. On September 11, 1941, in the ninth inning, the New York Giants left fielder singled. *Gordon,* who was making his major league debut, was walked in the fifth inning by Johnny Vander Meer with the bases loaded and then scored on Billy Jurges double. Bob Carpenter yielded 4 hits, as the Giants defeated the Cincinnati Reds, at Crosley Field, 6-0. Gordon had 1,415 hits, 202 home runs and a .283 career batting average.

65. ▶ Red Ruffing. On September 21, 1928, the St. Louis Browns catcher debuted and had a single in 3 at-bats. Ruffing yielded 9 hits, as the Boston Red Sox defeated the Browns, at Sportsman's Park, 5-3. Jack Ogden took the loss. Ruffing hit a 3-run homer.

66. ▶ *Moe Berg.* Among the several languages he spoke or translated were Japanese and Sanskrit.

HALL
OF
FAME

67. ► In 1940, this Hall of Famer (selected in 1975) singled to enable *Richard Conger* to win his first major league game...?

ALL-STARS

68. ► This pitcher, who later managed the 1961 pennant-winning Reds, surrendered *Al Rosen's* first major league home run...?

1960-
PRESENT

69. ► In a 1960 game at the Los Angeles Memorial Coliseum, Ron Kline surrendered this Jewish catcher's only grand slam home run...?

1930-59

70. ► *Herbert Gorman* made his only major league appearance in this Chicago stadium...?

OLD-TIMERS
1857-1929

71. ► He is the only pitcher who ever hurled shutouts in both ends of a doubleheader...?

BASEBALL
MISCELLANY

72. ► This early twentieth century player was known as "The Yiddish Curver"...?

 (Answers next page.)

ANSWERS

67. ► Earl Averill. On April 22, 1940, the Detroit Tigers reliever debuted and hurled a scoreless eighth inning, allowing 1 walk and striking out 1 batter. In the ninth inning, Averill batted for Conger and hit a 2-run single. Al Benton relieved and protected the win, as the Tigers defeated the Chicago White Sox, at Comiskey Park, 6-5. Clint Brown took the loss.

68. ► Fred Hutchinson. On April 18, 1950, in the eighth inning on Opening Day at Municipal Stadium, the Cleveland Indians third baseman's homer scored Lou Boudreau. The Detroit Tigers defeated the Indians, in 10 innings, 7-6. *Rosen* hit a league-leading 37 home runs in his rookie season.

69. ► *Norm Sherry.* On May 31, 1960, in the sixth inning, the Los Angeles Dodgers catcher hit a home run. The Dodgers defeated the St. Louis Cardinals, 8-3. Stan Williams, with relief help from *Larry Sherry,* was the winning pitcher.

70. ► Wrigley Field. On April 19, 1952, in the seventh inning, Gorman batted for St. Louis Cardinals pitcher Willard Schmidt and grounded out in his only at-bat. Turk Lown yielded 4 hits, as the Chicago Cubs defeated the Cardinals, 8-1. Hank Sauer and Frankie Baumholtz homered for the Cubs.

71. ► *Ed Reulbach.* In 1908, in a doubleheader against the Brooklyn Dodgers, he pitched 2 shutouts. In his career, he had 40.

72. ► *Barney Pelty.* He was an early curve-ball pitcher.

HALL
OF
FAME

73. ► This Dodgers pitching great led the National League in ERA for 5 consecutive years...?

ALL-STARS

74. ► In 1971, Danny Breeden caught this Jewish hurler's no-hitter...?

1960-
PRESENT

75. ► This Jewish slugger holds the Washington Senators all-time record for most home runs by a left-handed batter in one season...?

1930-59

76. ► Redlegs pinch-hitter *Al Silvera* had his only major league hit in this stadium...?

OLD-TIMERS
1857-1929

77. ► This hurler, who won 247 games between 1909-1933, surrendered *Mike Simon*'s only major league home run...?

BASEBALL
MISCELLANY

78. ► This Jewish third baseman was nicknamed "Flip"...?

(Answers next page.)

ANSWERS

73. ▶ *Sandy Koufax.* His season records from 1962 to 1966 were 2.54; 1.88; 1.74; 2.04 and 1.73

74. ▶ *Ken Holtzman.* On June 3, 1971, *Holtzman* hurled the second no-hitter of his major league career. In the third inning, *Holtzman* was safe on an error and later scored on Glenn Beckert's single. The Chicago Cubs defeated the Cincinnati Reds, at Riverfront Stadium, 1-0. Gary Nolan was the losing pitcher.

75. ▶ *Mike Epstein* hit 30 homers in 1969.

76. ▶ Crosley Field, Cincinnati. On June 26, 1955, in the eighth inning of the first game of a doubleheader, *Silvera* batted for shortstop Roy McMillan and hit a 2-run single off Murry Dickson. The Cincinnati Redlegs defeated the Philadelphia Phillies, 16-5. Jackie Collum was the winning pitcher.

77. ▶ Jack Quinn. On September 15, 1913, in the first game of a doubleheader, the Pittsburgh Pirates catcher hit a home run. Quinn yielded 10 hits, as the Boston Braves defeated the Pirates, at Forbes Field, 6-5. George McQuillan took the loss.

78. ▶ *Al Rosen.*

79. ► This Jewish slugger played for Pittsburgh for only one season and led the National League in walks...?

80. ► Who was the Jewish infielder who had more than 2,000 career hits and won the American League batting crown in 1935?

81. ► In 1970, Bill Hands, a former 20-game winner, surrendered the hit which enabled this Reds Jewish pitcher to bat 1.000 for the season...?

82. ► This Giants Jewish catcher was behind the plate for *Harry Feldman's* first career shutout...?

83. ► In 1920, Patsy Gharrity caught this Jewish Senators only major league shutout...?

84. ► This Jewish Hollywood celebrity was part-owner of the Seattle Mariners from 1977 to 1979...?

(Answers next page.)

ANSWERS

HALL
OF
FAME

79. ► *Hank Greenberg* had 104 walks in 1947.

ALL-STARS

80. ► *Charles "Buddy" Myer.* In 151 games he had 215 hits for a .349 percentage.

1960-
PRESENT

81. ► *Bo Belinsky.* On May 18, 1970, in the third inning, Belinsky singled. The Chicago Cubs defeated the Cincinnati Reds, at Crosley Field, 12-5.

1930-59

82. ► *Harry Danning.* On September 21, 1941, in the first game of a doubleheader at the Polo Grounds, *Feldman* yielded 9 hits, as the New York Giants defeated the Boston Braves, 4-0. Jim Tobin was the losing pitcher. Giants outfielders *Morrie Arnovich* and *Sid Gordon* each had 1 hit.

OLD-TIMERS
1857-1929

83. ► *Al Schacht.* On April 19, 1920, *Schacht* yielded 9 hits, as the Washington Senators defeated the Philadelphia Athletics, at Shibe Park, 7-0. Scott Perry took the loss.

BASEBALL
MISCELLANY

84. ► *Danny Kaye.* The movie comedian is a life-long baseball fan.

HALL
OF
FAME

85. ▶ This Dodgers Hall of Famer was the losing pitcher of *Ken Holtzman*'s first major league victory...?

ALL-STARS

86. ▶ This Jewish slugger holds the Cleveland Indians all-time record for most home runs in one season...?

1960-
PRESENT

87. ▶ *Richie Scheinblum* hit 13 home runs during his major league career (1965-1974). This Giants 24-game winner surrendered his only National League homer...?

1930-59

88. ▶ *Sam Nahem* won his first major league game in this Philadelphia stadium...?

OLD-TIMERS
1857-1929

89. ▶ In a 1906 game, Eddie Hahn's single was the only hit allowed by this Browns hurler...?

BASEBALL
MISCELLANY

90. ▶ Which Jewish player was known as "Harry the Horse"...?

(Answers on page 48.)

HOLTZMAN CLOSES CAREER WITH A SHUTOUT

Kenny Holtzman looks to the catcher for the "sign."

Ken Holtzman, a lefthanded hurler, was a strong competitor. The author of two no-hitters, he was a mainstay on the Oakland A's staff that won three consecutive championships.

Ken was born to Henry and Jacqueline Holtzman on November 3, 1945, in St. Louis, Missouri. His parents came from St. Louis, where his father was in the machinery business. Ken attended University City High School, where he played baseball, graduating in 1963. He enrolled in the University of Illinois, and in 1965 was signed to a professional baseball contract by Bill Prince of the Chicago Cubs. He received a bonus, and reported to Treasure Valley (Caldwell, Idaho) in the Pioneer League, winning all four decisions, collecting 44 strikeouts in 27 innings, with an ERA of 1.00. He was sent to Wenatchee, Washington, in the Northwest League, appeared in eight games with a 4-3 record, and had 70 strikeouts in 59 innings and a 2.44 ERA.

His phenomenal start earned him a promotion to the Cubs in September. Ken recalls, "The first player I ever faced in the major leagues (Jim Ray Hart), hit a home run on the first pitch." He improved dramatically, retiring the next three batters, and began a very successful major league career.

Ken's first win came the following season when he defeated the Los Angeles Dodgers and Hall of Famer Don Drysdale. In 1967, he joined the National Guard, which limited his service, finishing 9-0 with a 2.52 ERA. Between 1965-71, Ken won 74 games for the Cubs, including no-hitters in 1969

No-hit #1

ATLANTA (N)				CHICAGO (N)			
	ab	r	h rbi		ab	r	h rbi
Alou, cf	4	0	0 0	Kessinger, ss	4	1	2 0
Millan, 2b	4	0	0 0	Beckers, 2b	4	1	1 0
H. Aaron, rf	4	0	0 0	Williams, lf	4	0	0 0
Carry, lf	2	0	0 0	Santo, 3b	4	1	1 3
Cepeda, 1b	3	0	0 0	Banks, 1b	3	0	0 0
Boyer, 3b	3	0	0 0	Hickman, rf	3	0	0 0
Dreier, c	2	0	0 0	Heath, c	2	0	0 0
Garrico, ss	2	0	0 0	Oliver, c	0	0	0 0
Niekro, p	2	0	0 0	Young, cf	2	0	1 0
T Aaron, ph	1	0	0 0	Holtzman, p	3	0	0 0
Neibauer, p	0	0	0 0				
	—	—	—	Total	29	3	5 3
Total	27	0	0 0				

Atlanta	0 0 0 0 0 0 0 0 0—0
Chicago	3 0 0 0 0 0 0 0 x—3

LOB—Atlanta 3, Chicago 4. HR—Santo (25)

	IP	H	R	ER	BB	SO
Niekro (L, 16—11)	7	5	3	3	2	4
Neibauer	1	0	0	0	0	0
Holtsman(W, 14—7)	9	0	0	0	3	0

Time—2:00. Attendance—37,514

(against the Atlanta Braves), and 1971 (against the Cincinnati Reds). He was traded to Oakland

No-hit #2

CHICAGO (N)				CINCINNATI (N)			
	ab	r	h rbi		ab	r	h rbi
Kessinger, ss	4	0	1 0	McRae, lf	3	0	0 0
Beckert, 2b	4	0	2 1	Helms, 2b	4	0	0 0
Williams, lf	4	0	1 0	May, 1b	3	0	0 0
Santo, 3b	4	0	0 0	Bench, c	3	0	0 0
Pepitone, 1b	4	0	1 0	Perez, 3b	3	0	0 0
Davis, cf	4	0	0 0	Foster, cf	3	0	0 0
Callison, rf	3	0	1 0	Bradford, rf	3	0	0 0
Breeden, c	3	0	0 0	Concepcion, ss	3	0	0 0
Holtzman, p	3	1	0 0	Nolan, p	2	0	0 0
	—	—	—	Ferrara, ph	1	0	0 0
Total	33	1	6 1	Gibbon, p	0	0	0 0
					—	—	—
				Total	26	0	0 0

Chicago	0 0 1 0 0 0 0 0 0—1
Cincinnati	0 0 0 0 0 0 0 0 0—0

E—Perez. DP—Chicago 1, Chicago 5, Cincinnati 3. SB—Kessinger, McRae.

	IP	H	R	ER	BB	SO
Holtzman (W, 3—6)	9	0	0	0	4	6
Nolan (L;. 3—6)	8	5	1	0	0	3
Gibbon	1	1	0	0	0	0

Wild Pitch—Holtzman. Time—1:55.
Attendance—11,751

for Rick Monday and contributed to the A's four West Division titles (1972-75), and three World Series Championships (1972-74). He was selected to the American League All-Star Squad (1972-73), and appeared in the 1973 game at Royals

Stadium. Ken won 77 games with the Athletics (21-13 in 1973), and was 2-3 with a 2.06 ERA in the Championship Series, and 4-1 with a 2.55 ERA in the World Series. He had four hits, including three doubles and a home run, in seven at-bats in World Series play.

Ken also played for the Baltimore Orioles (1976), and the New York Yankees (1976-78), before returning to the Chicago Cubs (1978-79). His thirty-first career shutout, and last major league win, was a three-hitter over the Houston Astros at Wrigley Field. He completed the 1979 season and retired. Ken says, "I had been in the major leagues for fifteen years. . . . I made up my mind before the 1979 season began that I was going to retire. . . . I had a business opportunity here in Chicago. . . . I really didn't look back. . . . The only time I missed the game was the following February when it was about twenty degrees below zero (in Chicago). . . . Everybody else was in Phoenix (Spring Training). . . . I guess I had hunger pains about going to Phoenix for a couple of months." In fifteen seasons, Ken appeared in 451 major league games, was 174-150 with a 3.49 ERA, and 1,601 strikeouts.

During the off-seasons, Ken returned to the University of Illinois, graduating with a degree in Business Administration in 1967. He has been employed as a stock broker, and now is in the commercial insurance business.

In his leisure Ken enjoys reading. He married Michelle Collons in 1971, and they have three daughters.

ANSWERS

85. ▶ Don Drysdale. On April 24, 1966, *Holtzman* yielded 3 hits in 6 innings and was relieved by Ted Abernathy. Don Kessinger's second-inning triple scored 2 runs. The Chicago Cubs defeated the Los Angeles Dodgers, at Wrigley Field, 2-0. *Holtzman* attended school and was available to the Cubs only on weekends.

ALL-STARS

86. ▶ *Al Rosen* hit 43 home runs in 1953.

1960-
PRESENT

87. ▶ Ron Bryant. On April 13, 1973, in the seventh inning, *Scheinblum* batted for Cesar Geronimo and hit a 2-run homer. The San Francisco Giants, with 3 runs in the eighth inning, defeated the Cincinnati Reds, at Candlestick Park, 5-4.

1930-59

88. ▶ Shibe Park. On October 2, 1938, in the first game of a doubleheader, the Brooklyn Dodgers rookie made his debut. *Nahem* yielded 6 hits, as the Dodgers defeated the Philadelphia Phillies, 7-3. Claude Passeau was the losing pitcher. Not content with his work on the mound, this versatile "rookie" pitcher also had 2 hits and 1 run batted in.

OLD-TIMERS
1857-1929

89. ▶ *Barney Pelty.* On July 4, 1906, in the morning game, Hahn led-off the ninth inning with a single. *Pelty* struck out 2 batters and walked 3, as the St. Louis Browns defeated the Chicago White Sox, at South Side Park, 3-0. Hall of Famer Branch Rickey caught the victory.

BASEBALL
MISCELLANY

90. ▶ *Harry Danning.*

91. ► In 1956, hurler Johnny Klippstein surrendered this Jewish pitcher's first of 75 career hits...?

92. ► This Orioles player was the starting pitcher for the American League in the 1980 All-Star Game...?

93. ► This player, a member of the 1969 New York Mets World Champions, caught for *Larry Yellen*, who was making his major league debut...?

94. ► In 1958, Johnny Romano caught this White Sox hurler's first career shutout...?

95. ► Byrd Lynn caught for this Jewish pitcher—who had 2 consecutive 21-game winning seasons—in his last game in the 1919 World Series...?

96. ► This Jewish catcher was a player/manager for the 1912 Boston Braves...?

(Answers next page.)

ANSWERS

HALL
OF
FAME

91. ▶ *Sandy Koufax.* On June 8, 1956, in the fifth inning, the Brooklyn Dodgers pitcher singled to right field. Klippstein yielded 7 hits, as the Cincinnati Reds defeated the Dodgers, at Crosley Field, 6-4. Reliever Clem Labine was the losing pitcher. *Koufax* had a .097 career batting average.

ALL-STARS

92. ▶ *Steve Stone.*

1960-
PRESENT

93. ▶ Jerry Grote. On September 26, 1963, *Yellen* debuted as the Colts starting pitcher and was relieved in the sixth inning after allowing 7 hits and 2 earned runs. In the eleventh inning, Joe Morgan singled off Roy Face and later scored on Bob Aspromonte's hit. The Houston Colt .45s defeated the Pittsburgh Pirates, at Colt Stadium, 5-4. This was the Colts' seventh consecutive victory.

1930-59

94. ▶ *Barry Latman.* On September 26, 1958, Johnny Callison's sixth-inning sacrifice fly scored Romano with the only run of the game. *Latman* contained the Kansas City Athletics sluggers to only 3 hits, as his Chicago White Sox defeated the Athletics, at Comiskey Park, 1-0. Bob Grim took the loss.

OLD-TIMERS
1857-1929

95. ▶ *Erskine Mayer.* On October 6, 1919, in the ninth inning of the fifth game, *Mayer* relieved White Sox hurler Lefty Williams and allowed 1 unearned run. The Cincinnati Reds defeated the Chicago White Sox, in Chicago, 5-0.

BASEBALL
MISCELLANY

96. ▶ *Johnny Kling.* He played for several Chicago Cubs Pennant winning teams.

HALL
OF
FAME

97. ► In 1940, this Indians Hall of Famer surrendered *Hank Greenberg*'s league-leading fiftieth and last double of the season...?

ALL-STARS

98. ► This hurler, a member of the 1939-1940 Champion Cincinnati Reds, was the losing pitcher of *Harry Feldman*'s last major league victory...?

1960-
PRESENT

99. ► *Richie Scheinblum* made his major league debut in this Kansas City stadium...?

1930-59

100. ► He was the Jewish slugger who holds the Boston Braves all-time record for most grand slam homers in one season...?

OLD-TIMERS
1857-1929

101. ► Jack Lynch surrendered this nineteenth-century Jewish player's first career home run...?

BASEBALL
MISCELLANY

102. ► Who was the Jewish owner of the Boston Braves who signed Babe Ruth to his last major league contract...?

(Answers next page.)

ANSWERS

97. ▶ Bob Feller. On September 27, 1940, in the second inning, *Greenberg* doubled. Floyd Giebell yielded 6 hits, as the Detroit Tigers defeated the Cleveland Indians, at Municipal Stadium, 2-0. The victory clinched the pennant for the Tigers. Feller allowed 3 hits, including Rudy York's 2-run homer.

98. ▶ Paul Derringer. On September 8, 1945, Derringer and Feldman engaged in a pitching duel. *Feldman* yielded 8 hits, as the New York Giants defeated the Chicago Cubs, at Wrigley Field, 3-0. This was *Feldman's* 35th career victory and sixth shutout.

99. ▶ Municipal Stadium. On September 1, 1965, in the seventh inning, *Scheinblum* ran for Joe Azcue and later scored on Fred Whitfield's double off winning pitcher John O'Donoghue. The Kansas City Athletics defeated the Cleveland Indians, 4-3. Luis Tiant took the loss.

100. ▶ *Sid Gordon* hit 4 grand slam homers in 1950.

101. ▶ *Dan Stearns.* On July 13, 1883, in an American Association game, the Baltimore Orioles first baseman hit a home run. The New York Metropolitans defeated the Baltimore Orioles, in Baltimore, 9-4. Hardie Henderson was the losing pitcher.

102. ▶ *Judge Emil Fuchs.*

103. ► *Sandy Koufax* hurled his eleventh and last shutout of the 1963 season in this St. Louis stadium...?

104. ► In a 1966 game, this Pirates Cy Young Award winner surrendered *Art Shamsky's* fourth consecutive homer...?

105. ► In a 1975 game, Tom Veryzer had the only hit off this Athletics Jewish hurler...?

106. ► In 1933, Earl Whitehill walked this Jewish Indian 4 times in his debut to tie a record...?

107. ► He was the Jewish third baseman who in his only full season with the Boston Red Sox led the American League in stolen bases...?

108. ► The Jewish author of "Portnoy's Complaint" also wrote "The Great American Novel," a book with a baseball theme...?

(Answers next page.)

ANSWERS

103. ▶ Busch Stadium. On September 17, 1963, *Koufax* yielded 4 hits on the way to a win and his major league record for most shutouts by a lefthanded pitcher. The Los Angeles Dodgers defeated the St. Louis Cardinals, 4-0. Curt Simmons took the loss.

104. ▶ Vernon Law. On August 14, 1966, in the seventh inning, *Shamsky* hit a 2-run, pinch-hit homer. The Pittsburgh Pirates defeated the Cincinnati Reds, at Crosley Field, 4-2. On August 12th, *Shamsky* hit 3 consecutive home runs. Law took home the coveted Cy Young top-pitcher trophy in 1960.

105. ▶ *Ken Holtzman.* On June 8, 1975, in the ninth inning, Veryzer's 2-out double was the only hit off *Holtzman.* The Oakland Athletics defeated the Detroit Tigers, at the Oakland Coliseum, 4-0.

106. ▶ *Milton Galatzer.* On June 25, 1933, in the first game of a doubleheader, Whitehill yielded 5 hits and 5 walks, as the Washington Senators defeated the Cleveland Indians, at Municipal Stadium, 9-0. Following his 4 walks in the first game, *Galatzer* swatted 2 hits in the second game.

107. ▶ *Buddy Myer* stole 30 bases in 1928. He was hefty with his bat, averaging .303 in 1,923 games over 17 years.

108. ▶ *Philip Roth.*

HALL
OF
FAME

109. ► In 1937, *Hank Greenberg*'s 183rd run-batted-in gave this Indians hurler his only loss of the season. . . ?

ALL-STARS

110. ► In 1953, this Jewish third baseman was a unanimous choice for the Most Valuable Player trophy. . . ?

1960-
PRESENT

111. ► Jim Colborn surrendered this Yankees Jewish batter's first pinch-hit home run. . . ?

1930-59

112. ► In which stadium did Reds reliever *Robert Katz* make his major league debut?

OLD-TIMERS
1857-1929

113. ► Frank Owen surrendered this 1906 Jewish Batting Champion's first career hit. . . ?

BASEBALL
MISCELLANY

114. ► Who managed the St. Louis Cardinals in 1900 and later established a baseball statistical bureau?

(Answers on page 58.)

FORMAN SURPRISE UMPIRE

The U.S. Navy inter-squad baseball game was about to begin. The players were in the dugout, waiting. But the man with the black hat, chest and face protector was noticeably absent.

Al Forman was drafted to serve as an umpire that day.

And thus began a career as an umpire that has gone on for more than a quarter century.

All of which points up that sometimes careers are born of accidents, because there was nothing in Al's history to suggest a sporting career.

Born July 7, 1928, in Morristown, New Jersey, to Seymour and Mollie Forman, he attended high school in his home town and worked for 5 years at various jobs before enlisting in the Navy in 1950.

Even that accidental beginning did not suggest a life of calling out "Play ball."

After military discharge in 1954, he attended Fairleigh Dickinson University, where he obtained an Associate Degree in Business Management.

But the call of the diamond must have stirred a strong chord in the unskilled umpire.

He had a good grounding in the basics of umpiring by the time he graduated from the Al Sommers School of Umpires in Daytona, Florida, in 1956.

The newly acquired skill parlayed into an umpiring career that took him through the minors, a winter league, the majors, and finally the college ranks.

The Morristown, New Jersey, high school graduate worked in the Florida State League in '56, the Northwest League in '57 and '58—a league that covered Washington, Oregon and Idaho—and the Nicaragua Winter League in 1958. For the next two years, he stood authoritatively behind the plate in the Texas League.

Then came his stint in the majors, as a National League umpire.

"My first game as a home plate umpire was at Wrigley Field," he recalls.

"It snowed that day and stranded us in Chicago for two days."

During the next five years he had many memorable games.

"I worked the bases when Willie Mays hit 4 home runs in 1 game," he recalled from Kitty Hawk, North Carolina, where he now lives with his wife Eleanore and owns and manages a highly successful limousine service.

"I was also umpiring the game when Sandy Koufax hurled his third no-hitter, and was at home plate when Hall of Famer Ernie Banks hit his 300th career home run."

He was also one of the umpires

millions of television viewers saw untangle the Dodgers and Giants the day Juan Marichal belted Johnny Rosboro with a bat.

And Al was making the pronounced closed-fist signals for the New York Yankees during the '79 umpires' strike.

Following the 1965 season, his National League contract was not renewed.

Since 1966 he has done most of his umpiring in the college ranks. Each year he has suited up for work in the Eastern Collegiate Athletic Conference, and the NCAA, and has made eight appearances (including '84 and '85) in the College World Series in Omaha, Nebraska.

One thing is for sure...Al

After a lifetime in baseball, *Al Forman* still calls out "Play ball."

Forman will, as usual, call out "Play Ball" in a ball park, somewhere in the world of baseball.

RICHTER WAS THE FANS' MOST POPULAR PLAYER

Al Richter in retirement

This Minor League All-Star shortstop was twice selected as the Most Popular Player by the fans. "Each time I was given a new automobile," says *Al Richter*.

Al, the youngest of three children of Sol and Flora Richter, was born on February 7, 1927, in Norfolk, Virginia. His father, from England, was raised in New York, and employed as a Justice of the Peace while his mother came from Baltimore, Maryland.

Al graduated from Norfolk's Maury High School in 1945, where he played baseball, football and basketball before signing a contract with the Boston Red Sox. His baseball career was delayed when he was drafted, and served

(Continued on Page 98.)

ANSWERS

109. ► Johnny Allen. On October 3, 1937, in the first inning, Pete Fox doubled and scored on *Greenberg*'s single. Jake Wade yielded 1 hit, a single to Hal Trosky, as the Detroit Tigers defeated the Cleveland Indians, at Navin Field, 1-0. Allen lost his only decision after 15 consecutive wins.

110. ► *Al Rosen.*

111. ► *Ron Blomberg.* On August 13, 1972, in the seventh inning of the second game of a doubleheader, *Blomberg* batted for Fred Beene and hit a 2-run homer. The New York Yankees defeated the Milwaukee Brewers, at Yankee Stadium, 5-4. Beene won his first major league game.

112. ► Crosley Field, Cincinnati. On May 12, 1944, the Cincinnati Reds rookie retired the side in order during the eighth inning and then left the game for a pinch-hitter. Reliever *Harry Feldman* was the winning pitcher, as the New York Giants defeated the Reds, 5-3. Ed Huesser took the loss. *Katz* appeared in 6 games and lost his only decision.

113. ► *George Stone.* On April 15, 1905, the St. Louis Browns left fielder singled and scored 1 run. Owen yielded 8 hits, as the Chicago White Sox defeated the Browns, at South Side Park, in 11 innings, 3-2. Fred Glade was the losing pitcher. *Stone* won the 1906 American League Batting Championship with a .358 average.

114. ► *Louis Heilbroner.* In 1910 he published the **Baseball Blue Book.**

115. ▶ This Scotsman was *Sandy Koufax'* first major league strikeout...?

116. ▶ In 1925, Vic Aldridge surrendered this Senators Jewish batter's first World Series hit...?

117. ▶ In 1970, Moe Drabowsky surrendered a grand slam homer to this Jewish slugger...?

118. ▶ *Hy Cohen* made his major league debut in this St. Louis stadium...?

119. ▶ He was the Jewish hurler who won 14 consecutive games for the Chicago Cubs...?

120. ▶ Which Jewish umpire worked in the 1934 All-Star Game?

(Answers next page.)

ANSWERS

115. ▶ Bobby Thomson. On June 24, 1955, in the fifth inning with the bases loaded, *Koufax* fanned Thomson. It was not enough for a win as Lew Burdette had given up 9 hits, as the Milwaukee Braves defeated the Brooklyn Dodgers, at County Stadium, 8-2. *Koufax* followed that strikeout with another 2,395 career strikeouts.

116. ▶ *Buddy Myer.* On October 8, 1925, in the second game, *Myer* entered the game as a pinch-runner and in the ninth inning singled for his first hit. The Pittsburgh Pirates defeated the Washington Senators, at Forbes Field, 3-2.

117. ▶ *Mike Epstein.* On June 19, 1970, in the first game of a doubleheader, the Washington Senators first baseman hit a 2-run homer off Jim Palmer in the first inning, a grand slam off Drabowsky in the seventh inning, and a 2-run single off Pete Richert in the ninth inning. Palmer was the winning pitcher, as the Baltimore Orioles defeated the Senators, at Memorial Stadium, 12-10.

118. ▶ Busch Stadium. On April 17, 1955, in the second game of a doubleheader, the St. Louis Cardinals scored 10 runs in the first inning. Harry Perkowski did not retire a batter and was relieved by *Cohen* who allowed 12 hits and 8 runs in 7 innings. Larry Jackson yielded 4 hits, as the Cardinals defeated the Chicago Cubs, 14-1.

119. ▶ *Ed Reulbach* won 14 consecutive games in 1909.

120. ▶ *Dolly Stark.*

HALL
OF
FAME

121. ▶ In 1923, *Louis Rosenberg* debuted against this Hall of Fame Yankee pitcher...?

ALL-STARS

122. ▶ He was the Indians Jewish third baseman who hit 4 grand slam homers in 1951...?

1960-
PRESENT

123. ▶ Ernie McAnally surrendered this Braves Jewish outfielder's only home run of the 1973 season...?

1930-59

124. ▶ In 1937, who was the pitcher that yielded *Harry Chozen*'s only major league hit?

OLD-TIMERS
1857-1929

125. ▶ This Cubs Jewish catcher was behind the plate during Bob Wicker's 1904 no-hitter...?

BASEBALL
MISCELLANY

126. ▶ Under the ownership of this Jewish sports enthusiast, the Pittsburgh Pirates won 6 pennants between the years 1900 to 1932...?

     (Answers next page.)

ANSWERS

HALL
OF
FAME

121. ▶ Herb Pennock. On May 22, 1923, in the fifteenth inning, Babe Ruth hit a 2-run homer off Mike Cvengros. *Rosenberg* batted for Cvengros and was retired. Pennock yielded 4 hits, as the New York Yankees defeated the Chicago White Sox, at Comiskey Park, 3-1.

ALL-STARS

122. ▶ *Al Rosen.*

1960-
PRESENT

123. ▶ *Norm Miller.* On July 13, 1973, in the second inning of the second game of a doubleheader, *Miller* hit a 3-run homer. In the third inning, his sacrifice fly scored another run. Carl Morton was the winning pitcher, as the Atlanta Braves defeated the Montreal Expos, at Atlanta Stadium, 15-6. During the season, *Miller* was traded by the Houston Astros to the Braves. Due to injuries, he appeared in 12 games with 3 hits and 6 runs batted in.

1930-59

124. ▶ Wayne LaMaster. On September 21, 1937, in the second game of a doubleheader, the Cincinnati Reds catcher singled in 4 plate appearances. *Chozen* caught Joe Cascarella and Bill Hallahan, the National League's starting pitcher in the 1933 All-Star Game. LaMaster yielded 8 hits, as the Philadelphia Phillies defeated the Reds, at Crosley Field, 10-1.

OLD-TIMERS
1857-1929

125. ▶ *Johnny Kling.* On June 11, 1904, Wicker allowed only 1 hit, a tenth inning single by Sam Mertes. Frank Chance singled in the twelfth inning and later scored on Johnny Evers' hit. The Chicago Cubs defeated the New York Giants, at the Polo Grounds, 1-0. Joe McGinnity lost his first game in 13 decisions.

BASEBALL
MISCELLANY

126. ▶ *Barney Dreyfuss.*

HALL
OF
FAME

127. ► This Hall of Famer's grand slam home run on the last day of the 1945 season enabled the Detroit Tigers to clinch the American League pennant . . . ?

ALL-STARS

128. ► Which Mets Jewish outfielder batted .538 in the first National League Championship Series?

1960-
PRESENT

129. ► In 1980, Rick Dempsey caught this hurler's only shutout of his Cy Young Award winning season . . . ?

1930-59

130. ► In 1951, Gus Niarhos caught a 17-inning night game, the longest in American League history. This White Sox Jewish player hurled the complete game . . . ?

OLD-TIMERS
1857-1929

131. ► Highlanders' third baseman *Phil Cooney* made his only major league appearance in this stadium . . . ?

BASEBALL
MISCELLANY

132. ► He was the Jewish former Senators pitcher who was an American League coach in the 1934 All-Star Game . . . ?

(Answers next page.)

ANSWERS

HALL
OF
FAME

127. ► *Hank Greenberg.* On September 30, 1945, in the ninth inning of the first game of a doubleheader, *Greenberg*'s homer off Nelson Potter scored Red Borom, Skeeter Webb and Doc Cramer. The Detroit Tigers defeated the St. Louis Browns, at Sportsman's Park, 6-3.

ALL-STARS

128. ► *Art Shamsky.*

1960-
PRESENT

129. ► *Steve Stone.* On June 21, 1980, the Baltimore Orioles pitcher won his seventh consecutive game and ninth victory of the season. *Stone* struck out 7 batters and yielded 5 hits, as the Orioles defeated the Seattle Mariners, at Memorial Stadium, 9-0. Dave Roberts took the loss.

1930-59

130. ► *Saul Rogovin.* On July 12, 1951, in the second game of a doubleheader, *Rogovin* yielded 12 hits, including a seventeenth-inning single to Lou Boudreau who later scored the winning run. Ellis Kinder was the winning pitcher, as the Boston Red Sox defeated the Chicago White Sox, at Comiskey Park, 5-4. Rogovin had 3 hits, including a double.

OLD-TIMERS
1857-1929

131. ► American League Park, New York. On September 27, 1905, *Cooney* replaced injured New York Highlanders third baseman Joe Yeager. He had no hits in 3 at-bats and handled 3 chances in the field without an error. Harry Howell yielded 5 hits, as the St. Louis Browns defeated the Highlanders, 7-2. Ambrose Puttman was the losing pitcher.

BASEBALL
MISCELLANY

132. ► *Al Schacht.*

HALL
OF
FAME

133. ► This Twins Cy Young Award winner surrendered *Sandy Koufax'* only World Series hit...?

ALL-STARS

134. ► This Jewish Senator was selected to the 1935 and 1937 All-Star Team...?

1960-
PRESENT

135. ► In a 1980 game, *Rod Carew's* single was the only hit off this White Sox Jewish hurler...?

1930-59

136. ► In 1930, pitcher Wes Ferrell allowed this Yankees Jewish slugger his only major league grand slam home run...?

OLD-TIMERS
1857-1929

137. ► *Ed Reulbach* made his major league debut in this New York stadium...?

BASEBALL
MISCELLANY

138. ► This Jewish owner of the New York Giants (1895-1902) signed Hall of Famer John McGraw to manage the team...?

        (Answers on page 68.)

BILL STARR PURCHASES SAN DIEGO PADRES

A syndicate including former Padre Bill Starr purchased the San Diego Padres today.

Starr will assume the reins as chief executive.

Those cold facts, set in print in 1944, do not tell the story behind *Bill Starr's* playing career in professional baseball, nor do they hint at what the nephew of an Orthodox rabbi from Russia would go on to accomplish in the big business side of baseball.

Born February 16, 1911, in Brooklyn, New York, to Isaac and Esther, he attended Joseph Medill High School in Chicago. His parents, natives of Russia, had met and married in New York before settling in the Midwest.

His father and his uncle had rabbinical training but, instead of following their tradition, early in life he decided to become a professional baseball player, influenced by the 1919 Chicago White Sox scandal.

(It was determined that 8 members of the White Sox had 'thrown' the 1919 World Series to the Cincinnati Reds.)

Bill wanted to help make the sport of baseball a clean one.

He had to wait 11 years for a chance to do this, when he put his signature on a baseball contract. That year, at age 20, he signed a professional contract and caught

Bill Starr: From baseball player to baseball owner.

for Lincoln in the Nebraska State League.

The next year he put on a mask for pennant-winning Norfolk in the Nebraska State League, and followed that playing a season with pennant-winning St. Joseph, Missouri, in the Western League.

In 1935, he caught for Albany, New York, in the International League and Harrisburg in the New York-Pennsylvania League.

Later that season, he had his first chance in the uniform of the Washington Senators.

His season with the Senators resulted in 12 games and 5 hits in 24 at bats.

Having had a taste of the majors, and having opened his eyes to the extraordinary potential in baseball ownership, he played for Chattanooga in the Southern Association and also for Albany, New York, then made the trip to the West Coast and the San Diego Padres.

At that time, they were still in the Pacific Coast League. He played with them for 3 years, then retired from baseball to operate his own private credit and collection agency.

Bill "Chick" Starr proved that some professional ballplayers make good businessmen and that the love of baseball is enduring—

when he looked around for a sound financial investment, after running his own extremely successful company, he chose buying the Padres.

From '44 through '55 he ran the Padres and directed them to the Pacific Coast League championship (1954).

During his tenure, he sold Tom Alston to the St. Louis Cardinals for what was, at that time, the highest price paid for a minor leaguer—$135,000 and 4 players, among whom were Dick Sisler, Eddie Erautt and Harry Elliott. This bold and astute business deal resulted in the league championship. Elliott also went on to win the batting crown.

During his ownership of the Padres, his managers included Pepper Martin, Lefty O'Doul and Bucky Harris, as well as coach Jimmy Reese ('48-60).

Since those days Bill, who has four children and nine grandchildren, has spent his time developing real estate—condominiums, shopping centers, etc.

Now, if another team were for sale . . .

67

ANSWERS

133. ▶ Jim Perry. On October 11, 1965, in the seventh inning of the fifth game, winning pitcher *Koufax'* 2-out single scored Ron Fairly. From the mound, *Koufax* yielded 4 hits, as the Los Angeles Dodgers defeated the Minnesota Twins, at Dodger Stadium, 7-0.

ALL-STARS

134. ▶ *Buddy Myer.*

1960-
PRESENT

135. ▶ *Ross Baumgarten.* On July 2, 1980, Carew led off the seventh inning with a single to stop the no-hitter. All told, *Baumgarten* walked 1 and fanned 5, as the Chicago White Sox defeated the California Angels, at Comiskey Park, 1-0. Frank Tanana took the loss.

1930-59

136. ▶ *Jimmy Reese.* On June 29, 1930, in the fifth inning, the New York Yankees Jewish second baseman homered. Red Ruffing was the winning pitcher, as the Yankees defeated the Cleveland Indians, at Yankee Stadium, 7-6. During that season, Reese had 3 home runs, 65 hits and a .346 batting average.

OLD-TIMERS
1857-1929

137. ▶ Polo Grounds. On May 16, 1905, *Reulbach* surrendered 4 hits in losing his first decision. Red Ames yielded 2 hits, as the New York Giants defeated the Chicago Cubs, 4-0. *Johnny Kling* was behind the plate for Reulbach's first game.

BASEBALL
MISCELLANY

138. ▶ *Andrew Freedman.*

HALL
OF
FAME

139. ▶ *Moe Solomon*'s major league career consists of 2 games, 3 hits and a .375 batting average. His first hit scored this Giants Hall of Famer, nicknamed "The Fordham Flash"...?

ALL-STARS

140. ▶ In a 1952 game, *Al Rosen* hit 3 home runs in this Philadelphia stadium...?

1960-
PRESENT

141. ▶ In 1968, this Astros Jewish batter scored the only run in a 24-inning game...?

1930-59

142. ▶ Who was the Jewish hurler, born in France, that won only one major league game?

OLD-TIMERS
1857-1929

143. ▶ This Jewish nineteenth-century third baseman played on 4 consecutive pennant winning teams...?

BASEBALL
MISCELLANY

144. ▶ He was the Jewish catcher known as "Noisy"...?

ANSWERS

139. ▶ Frankie Frisch. On September 30, 1923, *Solomon* made his debut as the New York Giants right fielder. In the tenth inning, Frisch and *Solomon* hit consecutive doubles off Joe Oeschger. The second blast ended the game. Rosy Ryan was the winning pitcher, as the Giants defeated the Boston Braves, at the Polo Grounds, 4-3. Three years earlier, Oeschger had been involved in a 26-inning game.

140. ▶ Shibe Park. On April 29, 1952, the Cleveland Indians third baseman homered off Alex Kellner, Harry Byrd and Tex Hoyle. *Rosen* had 4 hits and 7 runs batted in. Bob Feller yielded 18 hits, as the Indians defeated the Philadelphia Athletics, 21-9.

141. ▶ *Norm Miller.* On April 16, 1968, in the twenty-fourth inning, *Miller* singled off Les Rohr and later scored on an error. Wade Blasingame was the winning pitcher, as the Houston Astros defeated the New York Mets, at the Astrodome, 1-0. This was the longest night game in major league history.

142. ▶ *Duke Markell.* On September 27, 1951, Markell, from Paris, France, yielded 8 hits, as the St. Louis Browns defeated the Detroit Tigers, at Sportsman's Park, 7-4. Fred Hutchinson took the loss. Browns catcher Matt Batts hit a solo home run.

143. ▶ *Billy Nash.*

144. ▶ *Johnny Kling.*

145. ▶ *Hank Greenberg* debuted against this Yankees Hall of Famer...?

146. ▶ He was the Indians Jewish hurler who was selected to the American League squad for the second All-Star Game of 1961...?

147. ▶ In a 1970 game, Hal Lanier's single was the only hit allowed by this Cubs Jewish hurler...?

148. ▶ In 1951, Al Widmar surrendered this Jewish first baseman's only major league grand slam home run...?

149. ▶ This pitcher, who lost 19 consecutive games in 1916, surrendered *Sam Mayer's* only career home run...?

150. ▶ He was the Pulitzer Prize-winning author of *The Fixer*, who also wrote *The Natural*...?

(Answers next page.)

ANSWERS

145. ► Red Ruffing. On September 14, 1930, in the eighth inning, rookie *Greenberg,* who batted for Detroit Tigers pitcher Charlie Sullivan, was retired hitless but went on to baseball glory. Ruffing yielded 7 hits, as the New York Yankees defeated the Tigers, at Navin Field, 10-3. Earl Whitehill took the loss.

146. ► *Barry Latman.*

147. ► *Ken Holtzman.* On August 22, 1970, in the eighth inning with one out, the San Francisco Giants shortstop singled to center field. *Holtzman* allowed 3 walks, as the Chicago Cubs defeated the Giants, at Candlestick Park, 15-0. Gaylord Perry was the losing pitcher. Joe Pepitone and Billy Williams hit home runs.

148. ► *Lou Limmer.* On June 4, 1951, in the fifth inning, the Philadelphia Athletics first baseman hit a home run scoring Al Clark, Gus Zernial and Dave Philley. Bobby Shantz was the winning pitcher, as the Athletics defeated the St. Louis Browns, at Sportsman's Park, 7-6. Bill Kennedy took the loss.

149. ► Jack Nabors. On September 6, 1915, in the afternoon game, *Mayer,* the Washington Senators right fielder, hit a solo home run. Harry Harper yielded 3 hits, as the Senators defeated the Philadelphia Athletics, at Shibe Park, 5-0. The Senators won the morning game, 5-3.

150. ► *Bernard Malamud.*

151. ► This Twins batting champion scored the only earned run allowed by *Sandy Koufax* in the 1965 World Series...?

152. ► *Buddy Myer* won the 1935 American League batting crown in this Philadelphia stadium on the last day of the season...?

153. ► In 1980, Ferguson Jenkins' victory ended this Orioles Jewish pitcher's 14-game winning streak...?

154. ► Ruben Gomez surrendered this Pirates Jewish outfielder's only career grand slam home run...?

155. ► He was the Jewish pitcher who was Newark's only 20-game winner in the Federal League...?

156. ► This early twentieth century hurler was nicknamed "Klondike"...?

(Answers next page.)

ANSWERS

151. ► Tony Oliva. On October 7, 1965, in the sixth inning of the second game, Zoilo Versalles reached base on an error and scored on Oliva's double. Harmon Killebrew's single scored Oliva. Jim Kaat yielded 7 hits, as the Minnesota Twins defeated the Los Angeles Dodgers, at Metropolitan Stadium, 5-1.

152. ► Shibe Park. On September 29, 1935, the Washington Senators second baseman had 4 hits in 5 at bats and won the title with a .349 average. The Philadelphia Athletics defeated the Senators, 11-8. Bill Dietrich was the winning pitcher. Cleveland's Joe Vosmik finished the season with a .348 average.

153. ► *Steve Stone.* On July 31, 1980, Stone hurled 3 innings and left the game trailing, 5-0. The Texas Rangers defeated the Baltimore Orioles, at Arlington Stadium, 7-4.

154. ► *Cal Abrams.* On September 20, 1953, *Abrams'* fourth-inning homer scored Dick Smith, Nick Koback and Bob Friend. Friend yielded 8 hits, as the Pittsburgh Pirates defeated the New York Giants, at the Polo Grounds, 8-4.

155 ► *Ed Reulbach.*

156. ► *Harry Kane.*

157. ► *Al Rosen* pinch-hit for this ageless Hall of Famer in the 1948 World Series...?

158. ► This Cubs hurler, known as "Big Bill," surrendered *Hank Greenberg*'s only All-Star Game hit...?

159. ► In 1978, Mike Colbern caught this White Sox Jewish hurler's first major league shutout...?

160. ► In 1955, Andy Seminick caught this Phillies Jewish pitcher's first National League victory...?

161. ► This Jewish catcher led the National League in fielding percentage during 4 consecutive years (1902-1905)...?

162. ► Born James Erskine, this Jewish pitcher was a 20-game winner for two consecutive years...?

(Answers on page 78.)

RATZER DELAYS BASEBALL CAREER
AND SITS *SHIVA*

Steve Ratzer's career began with a tragedy but ended gloriously.

Steve Ratzer's baseball career began in the worst way. Waiting in the Calgary, Canada, airport for a connecting flight to Lethbridge, Alberta, he learned of his father's death from a heart attack.

He was faced with a decision that could have confounded many a young man on his way to his first job.

His flight was to begin his baseball career with Lethbridge of the Pioneer League, the first assignment since being signed by the Montreal Expos following gradua-

tion from St. John's University in 1975.

Steve returned to New York and sat *shiva* for his father, an executive vice-president of National Shirt Shops.

Only then could he responsibly pick up his career.

Steve, the oldest of 3 children of Aaron and Florence Ratzer, was born September 9, 1953, in Paterson, New Jersey. He was raised in New York City, and in his senior year at Flushing's John Bowne High School was selected to the All-City Baseball Team.

His career found him constantly boarding planes. After signing with the Expos, he boarded a plane for the minors—in Lethbridge he had a 3-4 record; the following seasons he traveled to West Palm Beach in the Florida State League, where he was 8-8, then 3-3, and Quebec City in the Eastern League, 3-6 and a 1.48 ERA.

For the next three years his plane ticket took him to Denver. In '80 he was the American Association Pitcher of the Year (15-4 record with a 3.59 ERA).

At the end of '80 he was promoted to the Expos, appearing in one game.

He played 12 games for the Expos in 1981 and was 1-1, then

went back to Denver (where he was 7-3).

"The last pitch I threw in the majors was hit for a home run by Pedro Guerrero," he said.

A trade to the New York Mets resulted in his appearing for Tidewater in the International League. He compiled an 11-7 record and was the "Rolaids Minor League Fireman of the Year,"

He was soon back with Denver, this time via a trade to the Chicago White Sox.

However, for 6 years during his travels from the majors to the minors, Steve played winter ball in Venezuela and the Dominican Republic.

"In 1980 and '81, I pitched for the pennant-winners, Escogido ('The Chosen') in the Dominican Republic," he says.

"In 1980, I was 9-1 with 14 saves and was selected as Most Valuable Player."

He was the Most Valuable Pitcher in both seasons.

"At the end of the '83 season, I looked at my little girl, who was then 10 months old, and realized that I didn't know her."

Baseball was consuming so much of his time and energy that he decided enough was enough and he would retire to spend most of his time with his wife, Janet Eifert, and his three children.

He lives in the Denver area where he is the general manager of a restaurant and assistant regional supervisor for other restaurants.

His record began with a stumble but ended gloriously.

"I finished my career with 9 straight championship teams," says Ratzer.

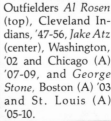

Outfielders *Al Rosen* (top), Cleveland Indians, '47-56, *Jake Atz* (center), Washington, '02 and Chicago (A) '07-09, and *George Stone,* Boston (A) '03 and St. Louis (A) '05-10.

ANSWERS

157. ► Satchel Paige. On October 10, 1948, in the seventh inning of the fifth game, *Rosen* batted for Paige and faced Boston Braves reliever Warren Spahn. He may have had dreams of glory, but instead popped out to the second baseman. The Braves defeated the Cleveland Indians, at Municipal Stadium, 11-5. Bob Feller took the loss.

158. ► Bill Lee. On July 11, 1939, in the fourth inning, the Detroit Tigers first baseman singled and scored, as the American League defeated the National League, at Yankee Stadium, 3-1.

159. ► *Ross Baumgarten.* On August 27, 1978, *Baumgarten* yielded 5 hits, as the Chicago White Sox defeated the Cleveland Indians, at Comiskey Park, 6-0. Paul Reuschel took the loss.

160. ► *Saul Rogovin.* On July 20, 1955, in the first game of a doubleheader, *Rogovin* yielded 5 hits, as the Philadelphia Phillies defeated the Cincinnati Redlegs, at Connie Mack Stadium, 6-0. Art Fowler was the losing pitcher. The Phillies were led by Seminick's 3-run homer and *Rogovin's* double and 2 runs batted in.

161. ► *Johnny Kling.*

162. ► *Erskine Mayer.*

HALL
OF
FAME
163. ▶ Which Dodger caught *Sandy Koufax'* first no-hitter?

ALL-STARS
164. ▶ This Tigers hero of the 1968 World Series surrendered *Mike Epstein*'s only Championship Series home run...?

1960-
PRESENT
165. ▶ In 1973, Mike Kekich allowed this Tigers Jewish outfielder's first major league hit...?

1930-59
166. ▶ He was the Jewish slugger who shares the New York Giants all-time record for most grand slam homers in one season...?

OLD-TIMERS
1857-1929
167. ▶ This 3-time no-hit hurler surrendered *Chief Roseman*'s first major league home run...?

BASEBALL
MISCELLANY
168. ▶ Who wrote the well-known baseball story *Bang the Drum Slowly*?

ANSWERS

163. ► Johnny Roseboro. On June 30, 1962, *Koufax* fanned 13 and walked 5, as the Los Angeles Dodgers defeated the New York Mets, at Dodger Stadium, 5-0.

164. ► Mickey Lolich. On October 11, 1972, in the seventh inning of the fourth game at Tiger Stadium, the Oakland Athletics first baseman hit a solo home run. John Hiller was the winning pitcher, as the Detroit Tigers defeated the Athletics, in ten innings, 4-3.

165. ► *Dick Sharon.* On May 14, 1973, in the eighth inning, the Detroit Tigers right fielder had a run-scoring double. Joe Coleman yielded 6 hits, as the Tigers blanked the New York Yankees, at Yankee Stadium, 8-0. Fritz Peterson was the losing pitcher.

166. ► *Sid Gordon* hit 3 grand slams in 1948.

167. ► Larry Corcoran. On July 4, 1882, in the afternoon game at Chicago's Lake Park, the Troy Trojans right fielder hit his only home run of the season. Pitcher Corcoran yielded 11 hits, as the Chicago White Stockings defeated the Trojans, in 14 innings, 9-5. Tim Keefe took the loss.

168. ► *Mark Harris.*

HALL
OF
FAME

169. ▶ *Bob Berman* appeared in one game as a catcher and caught this Hall of Famer, known as "The Big Train"...?

ALL-STARS

170. ▶ This Jewish catcher was selected to the National League All-Star Team 4 consecutive years (1938-1941)...?

1960-
PRESENT

171. ▶ In 1979, Barry Foote caught this Jewish hurler's 174th and last career victory...?

1930-59

172. ▶ In 1947, Earl Caldwell surrendered this Jewish third baseman's only major league home run...?

OLD-TIMERS
1857-1929

173. ▶ In 1905, Jack Taylor hurled 18 innings and Tully Sparks hurled 20 innings, both losing to this Jewish pitcher...?

BASEBALL
MISCELLANY

174. ▶ Who was the turn-of-the-century Jewish catcher known as "Broadway Aleck"?

(Answers next page.)

ANSWERS

169. ▶ Walter Johnson. On June 12, 1918, Johnson batted for catcher Val Picinich and doubled in the Washington Senators' 6-run ninth inning. *Berman* caught the last of the ninth inning, as Johnson revealed his ball was as sound as his bat and fanned 2, walked 1 and allowed only 1 hit. Stanley Reese won his only major league decision, as the Senators defeated the St. Louis Browns, at Sportsman's Park, 6-4. Urban Shocker was the losing pitcher. *Berman* was used as a pinch-runner in his only other major league game.

170. ▶ *Harry Danning.*

171. ▶ *Ken Holtzman.* On July 7, 1979, in the first game of a double-header, *Holtzman* hurled a 3-hitter for his 31st career shutout. The Chicago Cubs defeated the Houston Astros, at Wrigley Field, 6-0. Rick Williams took the loss.

172. ▶ *Mickey Rutner.* On September 13, 1947, in the eighth inning, the Philadelphia Athletics third baseman hit a solo homer. Bill Dietrich yielded 5 hits, as the Athletics defeated the Chicago White Sox, at Shibe Park, 9-2. Bob Gillespie was the losing pitcher.

173. ▶ *Ed Reulbach.* On June 24, 1905, at Robison Field, *Reulbach* yielded 15 hits, as the Chicago Cubs defeated the St. Louis Cardinals, in 18 innings, 2-1. On August 24, 1905, at Philadelphia Ball Park, *Reulbach* surrendered 13 hits, as the Cubs defeated the Philadelphia Phillies, in 20 innings, 2-1.

174. ▶ *Broadway Smith.*

HALL
OF
FAME

175. ► In a 1938 game, Pete Appleton surrendered this Jewish slugger's fourth consecutive home run...?

ALL-STARS

176. ► Stubby Overmire yielded this Indians
Jewish slugger's first major league
hit...?

1960-
PRESENT

177. ► This Jewish hurler was selected "The
Player of the Decade" (1960-1969)...?

1930-59

178. ► *Harry Shuman* made his major league
debut in which New York stadium?

OLD-TIMERS
1857-1929

179. ► In 1903, Joe Sugden caught this Jewish
hurler's first of 91 career victories...?

BASEBALL
MISCELLANY

180. ► This Jewish Hollywood producer presented *The Pride of the Yankees*...?

ANSWERS

HALL
OF
FAME

175. ► *Hank Greenberg.* On July 26, 1938, *Greenberg* homered in the sixth and eighth innings. His home run off Chief Hogsett gave the victory to reliever *Harry Eisenstat.* The Detroit Tigers defeated the Washington Senators, 6-5. On July 27, 1938, *Greenberg* hit a 3-run homer in the first inning off Monte Weaver and a 2-run homer in the second inning off Appleton. The Tigers defeated the Senators, 9-4. Roxie Lawson was the winning pitcher.

ALL-STARS

176. ► *Al Rosen.* On September 22, 1947, in the ninth inning of the second game of a doubleheader, *Rosen* batted for Ed Klieman and singled. He later scored on Hank Edwards' 3-run homer off Virgil Trucks. Klieman was the winning pitcher, as the Cleveland Indians defeated the Detroit Tigers, at Briggs Stadium, 7-6.

1960-
PRESENT

177. ► *Sandy Koufax.*

1930-59

178. ► The Polo Grounds. On September 14, 1942, the Pittsburgh Pirates reliever hurled 2 scoreless innings. Hal Schumacher yielded 6 hits, as the New York Giants defeated the Pirates, 6-1. Dutch Dietz took the loss.

OLD-TIMERS
1857-1929

179. ► *Barney Pelty.* On August 22, 1903, Sugden crouched behind the plate while Pelty allowed 8 hits, as the St. Louis Browns defeated the Boston Somersets, at Sportsman's Park, 2-1. Bill Dinneen was the losing pitcher.

BASEBALL
MISCELLANY

180. ► *Samuel Goldwyn.*

HALL
OF
FAME
181. ▶ In 1901, Jewish player *Broadway Smith* caught this Giants Hall of Famer, known as "Big Six," when he hurled his first career shutout . . . ?

ALL-STARS
182. ▶ In the 1959 World Series, Gerry Staley and Billy Pierce surrendered hits to this Dodgers Jewish pitcher in the same game . . . ?

1960-
PRESENT
183. ▶ Name 2 of the 3 Jewish players who appeared with the 1976 pennant winning New York Yankees...?

1930-59
184. ▶ *Al Richter* made his major league debut in which Boston stadium?

OLD-TIMERS
1857-1929
185. ▶ This nineteenth-century Jewish outfielder was the first St. Louis player to hit a home run . . . ?

BASEBALL
MISCELLANY
186. ▶ The Federal League's only batting champion was Jewish and was known as "Ty Cobb of the Feds" . . . ?

(Answers on page 88.)

JEWISH BASEBALL NEWS   **Bulletin**

WEINTRAUB RETIRES AT 38

"I was thirty eight when I quit," recalls *Phil Weintraub,* who ended his career with the New York Giants in 1945.

"I could still hit, but the running was too much for me."

Before he put his bat away, Phil had 407 hits in 1,382 at-bats, with 215 runs scored, 32 homers, 207 RBI in 444 major league games. His career batting average was .295.

Not bad figures for a ballplayer who first started on the mound 20 years earlier.

Phil, the third of six children of Israel and Rose, was born October 12, 1907, in Chicago, Illinois. His parents were originally natives of Kiev, Russia.

After leaving Tuley High School in Chicago in 1926, Phil went to work as a pitcher for Rock Island, Illinois, in the Mississippi Valley League.

The following seasons, he hurled for Waco in the Texas League and Tyler in the Lone Star League.

His work on the mound was poor but his batting average was good.

"Even though I could throw hard, I apparently was not destined to be a pitcher," he recalls from Southern California where he retired in '67.

"I was always a good hitter. Everybody thought they saw a great arm, and just overlooked the hitting."

After a 2-year hiatus taking care of the family auctioneering business, following the death of his father, Phil put on the pinstripes again.

This time he left the mound work to more accomplished pitchers, and concentrated on batting, playing at first base and in the outfield.

In 1930, Dubuque, Iowa, in the Mississippi Valley League was the first stop in the re-born baseballer's schedule. He missed the batting title by 1 percentage point.

The following seasons he played for pennant-winning Terre-Haute, Indiana, in the Three-I League; Dayton, Ohio, in the Middle Atlantic League, and Birmingham, Alabama, in the Southern Association.

Then it was time for Phil to take his batting prowess to the majors.

His first hit in the major leagues ('33) came as a member of the New York Giants against the Pittsburgh Pirates' Heine Meine at Forbes Field: he blasted a pitch high into the stands.

He continued this fierce approach to hitting the next season when in 101 games for Nashville in the Southern Association he had a league-leading .401 average. This was the first .400 average in the league in over 30 years.

For the remainder of that season, he played for the Giants, collecting 26 hits in 31 games and a .351 average.

In 1935, again a utility player, in 64 games he had 27 hits and a .241 average.

Weintraub spent '36 in the minors with Rochester. He dislocated his right shoulder sliding into a base and just missed the batting title. The following season he fought Frank McCormick of the Cincinnati Reds for first base and along the way collected 48 hits in 49 games, for a .271 average.

Before the season was over Phil was in the Giants uniform. In 6 games he had a .333 average before being shipped off to Jersey City in the International League.

A year later he was wearing the colors of the Philadelphia Phillies (100 games and a .311 average), but was sold to Minneapolis to help the financially-ailing Phillies out of their cash flow trouble.

After 2 seasons in the American Association (he made the All-Star Team in '40), and a brief retirement, Phil went to work for Los Angeles in the Pacific Coast League in '41.

With so much jockeying from majors to minors, it is difficult to keep his stats in mind.

"My overall average in the minor leagues was around .346,"

In a 20-year major and minor league career, *Phil Weintraub* twice donned the uniform of the New York Giants, '33-36 and '44-45.

he recalls.

It was .316 in 104 games when he next put on the Giants uniform ('44), including 11 RBI in 1 game and a grand slam; and .272 in 82 games the next year before retiring in mid-season.

He is married to Jeanne Holsman and they have two children and three grandchildren.

In 1982, Phil was elected to the Jewish Hall of Fame in Chicago.

ANSWERS

181. ► Christy Mathewson. On May 6, 1901, Mathewson yielded 5 hits, as the New York Giants defeated the Philadelphia Phillies, at the Polo Grounds, 4-0. Red Donahue took the loss.

182. ► *Larry Sherry*. On October 8, 1959, in the sixth and final game, the Los Angeles Dodgers reliever singled in the fifth and eighth innings. *Sherry* was the winning pitcher, as the Dodgers defeated the Chicago White Sox, at Comiskey Park, 9-3. Early Wynn took the loss. *Sherry* had 25 hits and a .169 career batting average.

183. ► *Ron Blomberg*, *Ken Holtzman* and *Elliott Maddox*, a convert to Judaism.

184. ► Fenway Park. On September 23, 1951, in the ninth inning, *Richter* batted for Red Sox catcher Les Moss and hit into a double play. Vic Raschi yielded 8 hits as he won his twentieth game of the season. The New York Yankees defeated the Boston Red Sox, 6-1. Chuck Stobbs was the losing pitcher.

185. ► *Lipman Pike*. On July 13, 1876, in the ninth inning, Pike, the St. Louis Brown Stockings center fielder, hit a solo home run off Tommy Bond. George Bradley yielded 5 hits, as the Brown Stockings defeated the Hartford Blues, at St. Louis Grand Avenue Park, 3-0.

186. ► *Benny Kauff.*

187. ► In 1926, *Andy Cohen* debuted and pinch-hit for this Hall of Famer, nicknamed "The Fordham Flash"...?

188. ► In 1945, this Dodgers Jewish outfielder finished third in the National League with a .325 batting average...?

189. ► In 1973, *Richie Scheinblum* had 5 hits in one game at this Kansas City stadium...?

190. ► In 1951, Phil Masi caught this White Sox Jewish hurler's first major league victory...?

191. ► This Jewish Cub was the only catcher to throw out Ty Cobb attempting to steal in a World Series game...?

192. ► Who is the author of the book with a baseball theme called *The Boys of Summer*?

(Answers next page.)

ANSWERS

187. ► Frankie Frisch. On May 31, 1926, in the ninth inning, *Cohen* singled off Philadelphia Phillies hurler Ray Pierce. Freddie Fitzsimmons yielded 9 hits, as the New York Giants defeated the Phillies, at Baker Bowl, 12-1. Ernie Maun was the losing pitcher.

ALL-STARS

188. ► *Goody Rosen.*

1960-
PRESENT

189. ► Royals Stadium. On July 28, 1973, the California Angels outfielder hit a 2-run double in the first inning and also had 4 singles. Aurelio Monteagudo was the winning pitcher, as the Angels defeated the Kansas City Royals, 19-8. Frank Robinson hit 2 home runs. In 1973, *Scheinblum* had 12 hits and a .222 average with the Cincinnati Reds and 75 hits and a .328 average with the Angels.

1930-59

190. ► *Marv Rotblatt.* On April 19, 1951, *Rotblatt* allowed 7 hits and was relieved in the seventh inning after walking the leadoff batter with a 9-1 lead. The Chicago White Sox defeated the St. Louis Browns, at Sportsman's Park, 13-5. Al Widmar took the loss. Al Zarilla and Eddie Robinson each hit 3-run homers.

OLD-TIMERS
1857-1929

191. ► *Johnny Kling.* On October 12, 1907, in the sixth inning, Cobb singled, continued to second on an error and was then caught stealing—*Kling* to Cubs third baseman Harry Steinfeldt. Three Finger Brown was the winning pitcher, as the Chicago Cubs defeated the Detroit Tigers, in the fifth and last game, in Detroit, 2-0. Cobb was caught attempting to steal home in the third game of the 1908 Series—relief pitcher *Ed Reulbach* to Kling to Steinfeldt.

BASEBALL
MISCELLANY

192. ► *Roger Kahn.*

HALL
OF
FAME 193. ► This White Sox Hall of Famer was catching when *Benny Kauff,* the Federal League stolen base champion, stole his only base in a World Series game...?

ALL-STARS 194. ► In the first night game at Baltimore's Memorial Stadium, *Al Rosen's* ninth-inning single was the first hit allowed by this Orioles hurler, nicknamed "Bullet Bob"...?

1960-
PRESENT 195. ► Pitcher *Steve Ratzer* debuted against this batter who singled for his 3,556th career hit...?

1930-59 196. ► *Louis Limmer,* in his second major league at bat, homered off this Yankee nicknamed "The Springfield Rifle"...?

OLD-TIMERS
1857-1929 197. ► Who was the Jewish hurler who completed 28 of 29 games in his 1905 rookie season?

BASEBALL
MISCELLANY 198. ► He was the former catcher who managed the California Angels from 1976 to 1977...?

(Answers next page.)

ANSWERS

193. ▶ Ray Schalk. On October 13, 1917, in the sixth inning of the fifth game, the New York Giants center fielder singled off Ed Cicotte and then stole second base. The Chicago White Sox defeated the Giants, 8-5.

194. ▶ Bob Turley. On April 21, 1954, in the ninth inning, *Rosen* slashed a 1-out single and Larry Doby followed with a home run. Bob Lemon yielded 8 hits, as the Cleveland Indians defeated the Baltimore Orioles, 2-1.

195. ▶ Pete Rose. On October 5, 1980, in the season finale, the Montreal Expos starting pitcher yielded 9 hits and 5 runs in 4 innings. Jerry White's 3-run homer in the tenth inning off Warren Brusstar ended the game. The Expos defeated the Philadelphia Phillies, at Olympic Stadium, 8-7. Charlie Lea was the winning pitcher.

196. ▶ Vic Raschi. On April 23, 1951, in the ninth inning, *Limmer* batted for Joe Tipton and hit a 2-run homer. Raschi gave up only 6 hits, as the New York Yankees defeated the Philadelphia Athletics, at Yankee Stadium, 5-4. Lou Brissie took the loss. In his first major league game, first baseman *Limmer* struck out.

197. ▶ *Ed Reulbach.*

198. ▶ *Norm Sherry.*

199. ▶ *Hank Greenberg* had 1,628 major league hits, including a single off this Hall of Famer, known as "The Splendid Splinter"...?

200. ▶ These two Jewish catchers were eligible to play in the 1933 World Series between the New York Giants and the Washington Senators...?

201. ▶ In 1970, Tom Egan caught this Angels Jewish pitcher's first major league victory...?

202. ▶ He was the "Double No-Hit" pitcher who surrendered *Cy Block*'s first career hit...?

203. ▶ Pitcher Pat Ragan and catcher Art Wilson were the battery when this Pirates Jewish pinch-runner stole two bases in one inning to tie a major league record...?

204. ▶ What do *Marilyn Monroe* and *Sammy Davis, Jr.* have in common with baseball's Jeff Newman?

ANSWERS

199. ▶ Ted Williams. On August 24, 1940, in the first game of a doubleheader, the Boston Red Sox outfielder made his only appearance as a pitcher and surrendered 3 hits in 2 innings. Tommy Bridges yielded 8 hits, as the Detroit Tigers defeated the Red Sox, at Fenway Park, 12-1. Joe Heving took the loss.

200. ▶ *Harry Danning* (New York Giants) and *Moe Berg* (Washington Senators).

201. ▶ *Lloyd Allen.* On September 30, 1970, *Allen* yielded 7 hits in 7⅔ innings and was relieved by Dave LaRoche. The California Angels defeated the Chicago White Sox, at Anaheim Stadium, 5-1. Tommy John was the losing pitcher.

202. ▶ Johnny Vander Meer. On September 7, 1942, in the second game of a doubleheader, the Chicago Cubs third baseman debuted and had a single, double and 1 run batted in. Hank Wyse was the winning pitcher, as the Cubs defeated the Cincinnati Reds, at Crosley Field, 5-3.

203. ▶ *Jake Pitler.* On May 24, 1918, in the ninth inning, Pittsburgh Pirates second baseman *Pitler* ran for Bill Hinchman and stole 2 bases. It wasn't enough as the Boston Braves defeated the Pirates, at Forbes Field, 6-3.

204. ▶ They are all converts to Judaism.

HALL
OF
FAME

205. ► This Jewish pitcher was elected to the Hall of Fame at 36 years of age . . . ?

ALL-STARS

206. ► In 1974, Andy Messersmith surrendered this Jewish hurler's only World Series home run . . . ?

1960-
PRESENT

207. ► In 1978, Alan Wirth yielded this White Sox Jewish slugger's only major league grand slam home run . . . ?

1930-59

208. ► This hurler, nicknamed "Jumbo Jim," surrendered *Max Rosenfeld*'s first career hit . . . ?

OLD-TIMERS
1857-1929

209. ► *Ed Wineapple* made his only major league appearance in this Washington stadium . . . ?

BASEBALL
MISCELLANY

210. ► Born James Hymie Solomon, this Jewish second baseman was a teammate of Babe Ruth . . . ?

     (Answers on page 100.)

YOM KIPPUR FIELDER'S ERROR

If he had been faced with the choice again, *Eddie Feinberg* would not have played on Yom Kippur.

Professional sports has often presented problems for the religious. Should Christians attend games on a Sunday, and should Jews go through the turnstiles on the Sabbath? Each man or woman makes a personal choice about buying that game ticket.

The athletes, on the other hand, rarely have such a choice. Their career role is to perform when called upon to do so. Most of them elect to advance their sporting careers by performing whenever their names are posted on the daily game roster.

There are certain religious Holy Days when members of any religion are faced with a soul-searching question.

The Philadelphia Phillies were scheduled to play a double-header in September 1938. This posed a problem for the three Jewish members of the team as that day was also Yom Kippur.

Morrie Arnovich and *Phil Weintraub* took the day off. *Eddie Feinberg* did not.

"I was young," Eddie recalls of that decision made shortly after he had become a member of the Phillies after floating around in the minors for two years.

The youngest of five children of William and Anna Feinberg, natives of Kiev, Russia, Eddie had dropped out of Philadelphia High School to sign a baseball contract with the Phillies in '37.

A utility fielder, he had played for Centreville, Maryland, a Phillies minor league farm team, in '37, in the Eastern Shore League. and Montgomery, Alabama, in the Southeastern League in '38.

At the end of that year, the 19-year-old Feinberg (born September 29, 1918) was promoted to the Phillies when he collected his first hit, a single, off St. Louis Cardinals hurler Mort Cooper.

The young man who lived for baseball began in '39 playing for St. Paul, Minnesota, in the American Association, before he was again promoted to the majors.

As a utility player, he often entered the game as a pinch-runner for infielder Pinky Whitney, and replaced him in the field.

In one game at Crosley Field he tied a major league record for shortstops, playing 12 innings without a fielding chance, while collecting 2 hits off Paul Derringer.

Then came Yom Kippur.

Young Eddie made the decision he was to regret for the rest of his life.

He played that doubleheader in Boston.

"God punished me," he recalled shortly before he died (April '86). He had retired to Florida in '82 after operating a restaurant in Philadelphia for many years.

"I went 0 for 8."

Eddie, the husband of Sally Goldstein, and the father of three children (seven grandchildren), would not have made the same decision if it had faced him again.

"I wasn't proud of my decision," he had said. "Believe me, I never did anything like that again in my whole life."

How much his Yom Kippur debacle affected his decision not to be sold by the Phillies in 1940 and to play instead for the semi-professional Brooklyn Bushwicks is hard to tell.

It did, however, affect how he regarded Yom Kippur for the rest of his life. He spent it as the Day of Atonement.

Nostalgia

Philadelphia stars, *Erskine Mayer* (top), Philadelphia (N) 1912-18, *Morrie Arnovich* (center), Philadelphia (N) '36-40, and *Chief Roseman*, Philadelphia (AA) 1887.

eighteen months with the U.S. Army Air Corps.

In 1947, Al began his professional career as a shortstop with Lynn, Massachusetts, in the New England League. The following two seasons were spent with Scranton, Pennsylvania, in the Eastern League, and in 1949, he was voted Most Popular Player by the fans.

For two seasons, Al played for Louisville, Kentucky, in the American Association, batting .321 in 1951 and receiving the "Look Magazine Award" as the Minor League All-Star shortstop. He received the award at Fenway Park at the end of the season when he was promoted to the Red Sox. He appeared in five games, collecting one hit in eleven at bats. Al debuted at Fenway Park as a pinch-hitter against Vic Raschi and hit into a double play. His only major league hit came on the last day of the season at Yankee Stadium when he singled off Spec Shea.

With Johnny Pesky, Lou Boudreau and Vern Stephens on the team, Al had few chances to play shortstop. For the next two sea-sons, he played for San Diego i the Pacific Coast League an Louisville, before returning to th Red Sox in 1953, when he ap peared in one game.

In 1954-55, Al played for Roch ester, New York (St. Louis Cardi nals Organization), in the Interna tional League. In 1955, he wa again selected as the Most Popula Player by the fans, before playing winter ball in the Dominican Re public, marking the end of hi baseball career.

During the off-season, Al at tended school, graduating from the University of Miami in 195. with a degree in Business Adminis tration. He has lived in the Nor folk area, working in real estat and in food merchandising. From 1958-64, Al had a fifteen-minute television show prior to the Sun day Game of the Week called "Spotlight on Sports."

Al is married to Ann Fulcher and they have one child. In 1983, he was voted into the Tidewater, Virginia, Hall of Fame. Al says, "They put a plaque by the door of the stadium along with the other Tidewater Hall of Fame members."

A PITCHER WHO COULD HIT

Izzy Goldstein, a right-handed hurler, was raised in an area of the Bronx that produced Hank Greenberg. Izzy was born June 6, 1908, in New York City. He is the oldest of three children of William and Ida Goldstein, who emigrated to the United States from Odessa, Russia. "We lived in the Bronx, about two blocks from Hank Greenberg." Izzy attended George Washington and James Monroe High Schools, and left in his senio year to pursue a baseball career.

He was a pitcher, and played semi-pro ball at Sea Cliff, Long Island, before signing a profes sional contract with the Detroi Tigers. In 1928, he hurled fo Wheeling, West Virginia, in the

A badly injured arm cut short the pitching career
of the Detroit Tigers Bronx-born *Izzy Goldstein*.

Mid-Atlantic League (14-9), and in
'29 and '30 for Evansville, Indiana,
in the Three-I League. In 1930,
Izzy was 16-9. The next year,
pitching for Beaumont in the
Texas League, he won 16 games
and was a teammate of Schoolboy
Rowe and Hank Greenberg.

Izzy began the 1932 season with
the Detroit Tigers, appearing in 16
games, winning three of five decisions, with a 4.47 ERA. He made
his debut in April at Detroit's
Navin Field, but was not involved
in the decision. In May he won his
first game, with relief help from
Whit Wyatt, as the Tigers defeated
the St. Louis Browns. Izzy finished
the season with Toronto in the International League, hurt his arm,

and after another year with Toronto, his pitching career ended.

Izzy was a good hitter. From
1934-38, he played semi-pro ball
as an outfielder with The Bushwicks, The Carltons and The Bay
Parkways in the New York City
area, until retiring from baseball
and entering the men's wear retail
business. He was in the U.S. Army
(1942-45), and served in the South
Pacific. Izzy retired in 1975, and
he and his wife Caroline Levine
reside in Florida.

Izzy Goldstein is recovering
from open heart surgery and a
stroke. He states, "Being seventy-
seven. . .it is flattering that people
still remember."

99

ANSWERS

205. ► *Sandy Koufax*, who in a 12-year career on the mound had a record of 165 wins, 87 losses and a 2.76 ERA.

206. ► *Ken Holtzman.* On October 16, 1974, in the third inning of the fourth game, the Oakland Athletics pitcher hit a solo home run. *Holtzman*, with relief help from Rollie Fingers, was the winning pitcher. The Athletics defeated the Los Angeles Dodgers, at the Oakland Coliseum, 5-2. Because of the use of designated hitters, *Holtzman* did not bat during the regular season.

207. ► *Ron Blomberg.* On September 19, 1978, in the eighth inning of the first game of a doubleheader, the Chicago White Sox designated hitter hit a grand slam homer. *Steve Stone*, with relief help from *Ross Baumgarten*, was the winning pitcher. The White Sox defeated the Oakland Athletics, at the Oakland Coliseum, 8-4.

208. ► Jim Elliott. On April 21, 1931, *Rosenfeld* debuted and replaced Johnny Frederick in center field for the Brooklyn Robins. He flied out in his initial at bat and doubled in the ninth inning. Elliott yielded 9 hits, as the Philadelphia Phillies defeated the Robins, at Baker Bowl, 7-3. Fred Heimach took the loss.

209. ► Griffith Stadium. On September 15, 1929, in the first game of a doubleheader, the Washington Senators reliever allowed 7 hits and 2 earned runs in 4 innings. Earl Whitehill yielded 6 hits, as the Detroit Tigers defeated the Senators, 16-2.

210. ► *Jimmy Reese.*

HALL
OF
FAME

211. ► This 22-game winner for the 1933 pennant-winning Washington Senators surrendered *Hank Greenberg's* first career home run. . . ?

ALL-STARS

212. ► In 1976, Steve Hargan allowed a pinch-hit grand slam homer to this Twins star. . . ?

1960-
PRESENT

213. ► Colts third baseman *Steve Hertz* debuted in which stadium?

1930-59

214. ► In a 1938 game, *Goody Rosen's* first inning lead-off single was the only hit allowed by this Giants hurler, nicknamed "Prince Hal". . . ?

OLD-TIMERS
1857-1929

215. ► Who was the Jewish outfielder who led the National League in home runs in 1877?

BASEBALL
MISCELLANY

216. ► He was the Jewish umpire who worked in the second 1962 All-Star Game. . . ?

(Answers next page.)

ANSWERS

211. ► Earl Whitehill. On May 6, 1933, *Greenberg* hit the first of his 331 career home runs. Whitehill yielded 12 hits, as the Wshington Senators defeated the Detroit Tigers, at Navin Field, 6-2. Carl Fischer took the loss.

212. ► *Rod Carew.* On September 9, 1976, in the seventh inning, *Carew* pinch-hit for Bob Randall and homered. Dave Goltz yielded 3 hits, as the Minnesota Twins defeated the Texas Rangers, at Arlington Stadium, 6-0. Jim Umbarger was the losing pitcher.

213. ► Colt Stadium, Houston. On April 21, 1964, *Hertz* replaced third baseman Bob Aspromonte and in his only plate appearance was fanned by John Tsitouris. Jim O'Toole was the winning pitcher, as the Cincinnati Reds defeated the Houston Colt .45s 10-5. Jim Owens took the loss.

214. ► Hal Schumacher. On April 24, 1938, Mel Ott hit a second-inning homer, as the New York Giants defeated the Brooklyn Dodgers, at Ebbets Field, 1-0. Van Lingle Mungo was the losing pitcher.

215. ► *Lipman Pike.* He hit 4 home runs.

216. ► *Al Forman.*

HALL
OF
FAME
217. ► In 1921, this Reds Hall of Famer fanned *Reuben Ewing* in his only major league at bat...?

ALL-STARS
218. ► A Jewish catcher was the Oakland Athletics' only player selected for the 1979 All-Star Game...?

1960-
PRESENT
219. ► Dodgers catcher *Norm Sherry* completed an unassisted double play in which stadium...?

1930-59
220. ► In 1945, this 22-game winner for the pennant-winning Chicago Cubs surrendered *Mike Schemer*'s only major league home run...?

OLD-TIMERS
1857-1929
221. ► This Phillies catcher (1902-1914) caught *Harry Kane*'s first victory and only career shutout...?

BASEBALL
MISCELLANY
222. ► A baseball writer managed Boston in the Union Association in 1884 and later helped to begin *Baseball Magazine*...?

(Answers next page.)

ANSWERS

217. ► Eppa Rixey. On June 27, 1921, in the sixth inning, *Ewing* batted for Tink Riviere and struck out. Rixey yielded 7 hits, as the Cincinnati Reds defeated the St. Louis Cardinals, at Sportsman's Park, 5-2. Roy Walker was the losing pitcher. In other games in this, his only major league season, *Ewing* appeared as a late-inning replacement at shortstop and as a pinch-runner.

218. ► *Jeff Newman.*

219. ► Memorial Coliseum, Los Angeles. On September 4, 1961, in the third inning, pitcher Juan Marichal struck out on a suicide squeeze and Jose Pagan, running from third base, was tagged out by the Los Angeles Dodgers catcher. Don Drysdale yielded 2 hits, as the Dodgers defeated the San Francisco Giants, 4-0.

220. ► Hank Wyse. On August 20, 1945, in the seventh inning, the New York Giants first baseman hit a 3-run homer. Van Lingle Mungo yielded 8 hits, as the Giants defeated the Chicago Cubs, at the Polo Grounds, 9-3. *Schemer* had 36 hits and a .330 career batting average.

221. ► Red Dooin. On September 27, 1905, *Kane* yielded 5 hits, as the Philadelphia Phillies defeated the St. Louis Cardinals, at Robison Field, 6-0. Jack Taylor took the loss.

222. ► *Jake Morse.*

223. ► In 1956, who became the first Jewish player admitted to the Hall of Fame?

224. ► Hall of Famer Red Ruffing surrendered this Senators Jewish shortstop's first of 2,131 career hits . . . ?

225. ► Doug Bird yielded this Jewish hurler's only major league hit (1978-1982) . . . ?

226. ► In 1932, Ray Hayworth caught this Tigers Jewish hurler's first career victory . . . ?

227. ► Ted Kennedy surrendered this nineteenth-century Jewish outfielder's only career home run...?

228. ► In 1956, this Cincinnati Redlegs Jewish Vice-President and General Manager was named "The Major League Executive of the Year" by *The Sporting News* . . . ?

(Answers next page.)

ANSWERS

223. ▶ *Hank Greenberg.* In a career that spanned 13 seasons (1930, 33-41, 45-47) he had 331 home runs and 1,276 RBI in 1,394 games with a .313 batting average.

224. ▶ *Buddy Myer.* On September 30, 1925, the Washington Senators shortstop singled for his first hit. Ruffing yielded 10 hits, as the Boston Red Sox defeated the Senators, at Fenway Park, 5-4. Win Ballou was the losing pitcher.

225. ▶ *Ross Baumgarten.* On July 1, 1982, the Pittsburgh Pirates pitcher singled in 2 at-bats. *Baumgarten* allowed 4 hits and 2 runs in 5 innings and was relieved by winning pitcher Enrique Romo. The Pirates defeated the Chicago Cubs, at Wrigley Field, 5-2. Bill Campbell took the loss. In view of the use of the designated hitter, *Baumgarten* did not bat for the Chicago White Sox (1978-1981).

226. ▶ *Izzy Goldstein.* On May 24, 1932, the Detroit Tigers rookie allowed 10 hits and 5 runs in 7⅓ innings and was then relieved by Whit Wyatt. The Tigers defeated the St. Louis Browns, at Navin Field, 6-5. Dick Coffman was the losing pitcher.

227. ▶ *Joe Strauss.* On July 8, 1886, in an American Association game, the Louisville Colonels left fielder homered. Tom Ramsey was the winning pitcher, as the Colonels defeated the Philadelphia Athletics, in Louisville, 14-6.

228. ▶ *Gabe Paul.*

229. ▶ This former Expos slugger was *Sandy Koufax'* record-setting 382nd and last strikeout victim of the 1965 season . . . ?

230. ▶ In a 1937 game, *Harry Danning* had 5 hits in this Philadelphia stadium . . . ?

231. ▶ This lefthanded reliever for the 1954 pennant-winning Indians became a starting pitcher for the Tigers and surrendered *Barry Latman*'s first major league home run . . . ?

232. ▶ Name 3 of the 5 Jewish players on the 1946 New York Giants?

233. ▶ This Hall of Famer, nicknamed "Chief," surrendered *Benny Kauff*'s first career hit . . . ?

234. ▶ This Pirates Jewish president from 1932 to 1946 brought Ralph Kiner to the major leagues . . . ?

     (Answers on page 110.)

ROSEN'S SUCCESSFUL HIKE

It was the Winter of 1930 in Toronto, Canada, and 18-year-old *Goody Rosen* was talking with a friend while neighbors were shooting a puck across the ice.

"I really want to make a living in baseball," the friend said.

"Well, let's do it then," replied Goody.

Such scenes are the stuff that grade B movies are made from, but in the case of Goody it was real, and it led to a baseball career that was far from grade B.

The two of them hiked their dream over 2,000 miles to Florida where they discovered there was no winter league.

Undaunted, Goody determined to stick it out until his dream became a reality.

A year later, he had tryouts with Little Rock and Memphis, with no luck, and had played for Rochester for 1 month.

"When they let me go, they said I was too small," he recalls.

The fifth of eight children to Samuel and Rebecca from Minsk, Russia, was not about to give up. He simply put on his hiking boots and went looking for another suitable team.

He tried out with Binghamton, New York, and reported to Stroudsburg, Pennsylvania.

The team folded after 6 weeks, but the hitchhiker did not fold away his dream. He kept trying.

Goody played twice for the Dodg ('37-39 and '44-46) before playing for New York Giants ('46).

His next hike was to Louisville in the American Association. The walking boots were retired for 5 years, as Goody found a home. Everyone discovered Rosen had talent as he was named to the All-Star team ('37).

He was promoted to the Brooklyn Dodgers and boarded a train whose destination was New York. In Brooklyn, in September 1937, he learned how to dodge the city's trolley cars as adroitly as he shagged balls on the fly.

In a doubleheader at Crosley Field, he debuted as a pinch-runner in the opening game. He collected 2 hits, 1 RBI and a stolen base in the second contest while playing center field.

That season, he played 22 games and had a .312 batting average.

In 1938, he batted .281, collected 133 hits, and broke up 2 no-hitters against Hal Schumacher and Bill McGee. He also led the National League outfielders in defense.

His dream now a reality, Goody settled down to the life of a professional baseball player. But fate would have it otherwise. A fierce slide resulted in torn ligaments above his left ankle, and Goody was on the road, again.

This time to Montreal in the International League. He was recalled by the Dodgers, fortunately, later that year.

Then came a 4-year stint with Syracuse before he was re-sold to the Dodgers. In 1944 he appeared in 89 games and had a .261 average.

The next year was his best. Goody Rosen finished with a .325

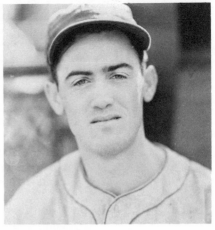

In 1938, *Goody Rosen* was the National League's leading defensive outfielder.

average and 197 hits.

During the 1946 season, Goody was traded to the New York Giants. In his first game for them, against the Dodgers, he had 5 hits in a double header.

But injury again altered his baseball career. Smashing into the base of a fence chasing a ball hit by Frank Gustine resulted in a banged-up arm and leg.

"Severe sprain of the outer clavicle. I couldn't raise my arm for 5 years."

Still that first 2,000-odd-mile hike had been worthwhile. In all, he had appeared in 551 games, had 1,916 at bats, 310 runs scored, 557 hits, 22 homers, 197 RBI, and a career batting average of .291.

In 1984, he was inducted into the Canadian Baseball Hall of Fame.

Today Goody and his wife of over 50 years, Mildred Rothberg, live happily in Canada. They have two children and four grandchildren.

And if one of them wants to get involved in a baseball career?

"I'd say, 'Let's go,'" says Goody Rosen enthusiastically.

109

ANSWERS

229. ► Mack Jones. On October 2, 1965, in the ninth inning, the Los Angeles Dodgers hurler fanned Jones for his thirteenth strikeout of the game. *Koufax* yielded 4 hits, as the Dodgers defeated the Milwaukee Braves, at Dodger Stadium, 3-1. Tony Cloninger took the loss. This game, *Koufax'* twenty-sixth victory of the season, clinched the pennant for the Dodgers.

230. ► Baker Bowl. On August 20, 1937, the New York Giants catcher had 5 hits, including a triple and 2 runs batted in. Dick Coffman was the winning pitcher, as the Giants defeated the Philadelphia Phillies, 13-6.

231. ► Don Mossi. On June 3, 1962, *Latman* relieved Cleveland Indians starter Pedro Ramos and in the third inning hit a solo homer. The Detroit Tigers defeated the Indians, at Tiger Stadium, 8-6.

232. ► *Morrie Arnovich, Harry Feldman, Sid Gordon, Goody Rosen* and *Mike Schemer.*

233. ► Chief Bender. On April 25, 1912, in the second inning, the New York Highlanders right fielder singled and later scored on Earl Gardner's hit. Bender yielded 10 hits, as the Philadelphia Athletics defeated the Highlanders, at American League Park, in 13 innings, 5-4. Russ Ford took the loss.

234. ► *William Benswanger.*

235. ► This Jewish first baseman had three 200-hit seasons...?

236. ► Which Yankee hurler won 21 games for 3 consecutive seasons (1949-1951) and surrendered the hit which enabled *Bud Swartz* to bat 1.000?

237. ► In 1980, *Steve Stone* hurled 12 consecutive hitless innings. This player, who previously played all 9 positions in one game, singled to break the string...?

238. ► In 1944, Fritz Ostermueller surrendered this Giants Jewish batter's only career grand slam home run...?

239. ► In 1905, Frank Roth caught this Jewish hurler's only shutout of the season...?

240. ► This Cincinnati Reds Jewish owner (1929-1933) acquired Ernie Lombardi and Paul Derringer, both contributors to Reds pennants in 1939 and 1940...?

(Answers next page.)

ANSWERS

235. ► *Hank Greenberg.* He had over 200 hits in 1934, 1935 and 1937.

236. ► Vic Raschi. On July 24, 1947, the St. Louis Browns reliever singled in his only at bat. Raschi gave up 9 hits, as the New York Yankees defeated the Browns, at Yankee Stadium, 14-5. Bob Muncrief was the losing pitcher.

237. ► Bert Campaneris. On August 19, 1980, in the eighth inning with one out, Campaneris singled for the California Angels first hit. *Stone,* with relief help from Tippy Martinez, won his twentieth game of the season. The Baltimore Orioles defeated the Angels, at Anaheim Stadium, 5-2. On August 14, 1980, *Stone* hurled a 2-hitter, allowing a second-inning homer to Reggie Jackson and a 1-out fifth inning single to Bucky Dent. The Orioles defeated the New York Yankees, at Memorial Stadium, 6-1.

238. ► *Phil Weintraub.* On July 18, 1944, in the third inning, the first baseman's homer scored Danny Gardella, Hugh Luby and Joe Medwick. Bill Voiselle yielded 3 hits, as the New York Giants defeated the Pittsburgh Pirates, at the Polo Grounds, 5-2.

239. ► *Barney Pelty.* On September 5, 1905, *Pelty* yielded 3 hits, as the St. Louis Browns defeated the Cleveland Naps, 6-0. Otto Hess took the loss. Hall of Fame pitcher Addie Joss made an appearance at third base for the Naps.

240. ► *Sidney Weil.*

241. ► This White Sox Hall of Famer, nick-named "Red," surrendered *Benny Kauff*'s first World Series hit . . . ?

242. ► In 1938, this future Cardinals Most Valuable Player surrendered *Eddie Feinberg*'s first career hit . . . ?

243. ► This Tigers All-Star was catching when *Mike Epstein* stole a base in a Championship Series game . . . ?

244. ► In 1930, Hank Johnson yielded this Jewish shortstop's first major league hit . . . ?

245. ► In 1908, this Cubs Jewish player caught *Ed Reulbach* when he hurled 2 shutouts in one day . . . ?

246. ► In 1928, the Washington Senators traded 5 players to the Boston Red Sox for which Jewish second baseman?

(Answers next page.)

ANSWERS

HALL
OF
FAME

241. ▶ Urban Faber. On October 11, 1917, in the fourth inning of the fourth game, the New York Giants center fielder hit an inside-the-park home run. *Kauff* added a 2-run homer in the eighth inning off Dave Danforth. Ferdie Schupp yielded 7 hits, as the Giants defeated the Chicago White Sox, at the Polo Grounds, 5-0.

ALL-STARS

242. ▶ Mort Cooper. On September 13, 1938, in the second game of a doubleheader, the Philadelphia Phillies shortstop singled in 2 at-bats. Cooper yielded 3 hits, as the St. Louis Cardinals defeated the Phillies, at Shibe Park, 3-2. Al Hollingsworth took the loss. Joe Medwick's homer won the game.

1960-
PRESENT

243. ▶ Bill Freehan. On October 12, 1972, in the second inning, Reggie Jackson scored and *Epstein* advanced to second on a double steal. Blue Moon Odom, with relief help from Vida Blue, was the winning pitcher. The Oakland Athletics defeated the Detroit Tigers, in the fifth and final game, 2-1. Woodie Fryman took the loss. Epstein stole 7 bases (1966-1974).

1930-59

244. ▶ *Jim Levey.* On September 17, 1930, the St. Louis Browns shortstop debuted and had 2 hits, including a 2-run double, and scored 2 runs. Rip Collins was the winning pitcher, as the Browns defeated the New York Yankees, at Sportsman's Park, 9-8.

OLD-TIMERS
1857-1929

245. ▶ *Johnny Kling.*

BASEBALL
MISCELLANY

246. ▶ *Buddy Myer.*

HALL
OF
FAME

247. ► This Hall of Famer, known as "Kid," won 360 games in his career and surrendered *Johnny Kling*'s only homer of the 1905 season . . . ?

ALL-STARS

248. ► In 1976, Mark Littell yielded this Jewish catcher's first career hit . . . ?

1960-
PRESENT

249. ► In 1982, *Ross Baumgarten* was the losing pitcher when this former Padres Cy Young Award winner won his 100th and last major league game . . . ?

1930-59

250. ► In 1930, Milt Gaston surrendered the only major league home run of this Indians Jewish player . . . ?

OLD-TIMERS
1857-1929

251. ► This nineteenth-century Jewish third baseman played in 3 different leagues . . . ?

BASEBALL
MISCELLANY

252. ► Who was the first Baltimore Orioles president (1901)?

     (Answers next page.)

ANSWERS

247. ▶ Kid Nichols. On July 4, 1905, in the second game of a doubleheader, *Kling,* the Chicago Cubs catcher, homered. Bob Wicker yielded 3 hits, as the Cubs defeated the St. Louis Cardinals, at West Side Park, 11-1.

248. ▶ *Jeff Newman.* On July 1, 1976, in the ninth inning, the Oakland Athletics catcher hit a 2-run single. Rollie Fingers was the winning pitcher, as the Athletics defeated the Kansas City Royals, at Royals Stadium, 5-2.

249. ▶ Randy Jones. On August 6, 1982, in the second game of a doubleheader, Jones was relieved by Neil Allen. The New York Mets defeated the Pittsburgh Pirates, at Three Rivers Stadium, 7-3.

250. ▶ *Jonah Goldman.* On May 5, 1930, in the seventh inning, the Cleveland Indians shortstop hit a solo home run. Gaston yielded 7 hits, as the Boston Red Sox defeated the Indians, at Fenway Park, 18-3. Willis Hudlin took the loss.

251. ▶ *Billy Nash* played in the American Association, National League and Players League.

252. ▶ *Sidney Frank.*

HALL
OF
FAME
253. ► This Jewish player fanned 12 consecutive times in 1955, a major league record...?

ALL-STARS
254. ► This Giants Jewish catcher had 3 hits in a 1937 World Series game...?

1960-
PRESENT
255. ► In 1971, this former Twins 20-game winner surrendered pitcher *Lloyd Allen's* only major league home run...?

1930-59
256. ► In 1938, Bill McGee hurled a one-hitter, allowing only a single to this Dodgers Jewish outfielder...?

OLD-TIMERS
1857-1929
257. ► In 1905, Tom Walker was the losing pitcher when this Cubs Jewish player hurled his first shutout...?

BASEBALL
MISCELLANY
258. ► Born Sammy Arthur Cohen, this Jewish infielder played for the Cincinnati Reds from 1921 to 1926...?

DANNING'S PERFECT BAT

It was the fourth game of the 1937 World Series, and the New York Giants were on the verge of elimination. (The New York Yankees had won the initial 3 games.) The Giants battled back to win their only game of the Series behind the 6-hit pitching of Carl Hubbell, 7-3. Catcher *Harry Danning* led the attack with 3 hits, including a double and 2 RBI.

Quite a day for most ballplayers, but not for Harry, who had many good days in his professional baseball career.

He is the fourth of six children of Robert and Jennie Danning who came from Riga, Latvia, and settled in Los Angeles, California, where Harry was born on September 6, 1911.

He yearned early to make a career somewhere on the diamond.

"I graduated from Los Angeles High in 1928" (the year his brother Ike played briefly with the St. Louis Browns). "They told me I was too young to play pro ball so I sold rugs and played semi-pro ball in Los Angeles until 1931."

"That was when a great friend of John McGraw, George Washington Grant, saw me play. He asked me if I'd sign with the Giants. I said 'yes'" he said recently.

He played for Bridgeport, Connecticut, in the Eastern League and then for Winston-Salem, North Carolina, in the Piedmont League.

On the strength of his .349 batting average for the first half of the 1933 season with Buffalo in the International League, he was promoted to the Giants.

For the next several years, he was the reserve catcher behind Gus Mancuso. When he put on the mask as the first-stringer in 1937, he gave the Giants power at the plate as well as behind it.

That season he batted .288 for the pennant-winning Giants and

Hits For The Cycle.

The box score:

PITTSBURGH (N.)	ab.	r.	h.	po.	a.	e.
Handley, 3b.	3	0	1	1	2	0
Elliott, rf.	4	0	2	0	0	0
Vaughan, ss.	2	0	0	0	0	0
F. Young, ss.	2	0	0	0	2	0
Fletcher, 1b.	4	1	1	10	0	0
Van Rob's, lf.	4	0	1	2	1	0
Gustine, 2b.	4	0	0	1	2	2
DiMaggio, cf	3	0	0	5	1	0
Davis, c.	1	0	1	2	1	2
Fernandes, c.	2	0	0	1	0	0
Bowman, p.	2	0	1	0	1	0
Lanahan, p.	0	0	0	0	0	0
Lanning, p.	1	0	0	0	0	0
Total	33	1	5	24	10	6

NEW YORK (N.)	ab.	r.	h.	po.	a.	e.
Whitch'd, 3b	5	1	1	2	1	1
Moore, lf	4	1	2	2	0	0
Seeds, cf	5	1	1	0	0	0
N. Young, 1b.	5	1	2	13	1	0
Danning, c.	5	3	4	5	1	0
Ott, rf	5	1	1	1	0	0
Jurges, ss.	4	1	1	1	0	0
Witek, 2b.	3	2	2	0	5	0
Schum'her, p.	3	2	3	0	5	0
Total	40	12	17	27	13	1

Pittsburgh ....0 1 0　0 0 0　0 0 0—1
New York ....0 0 3　0 7 2　0 0..—12

Runs batted in—Fletcher, Whitehead, Moore 2, Seeds, Young, Danning 3, Schumacher, Ott, Witek. Two-base hits—Danning, Ott. Three-base hit—Danning. Home runs—Fletcher, Danning. Stolen base—DiMaggio. Left on bases—New York 9, Pittsburgh 7. Bases on balls—Off Schumacher 3, Bowman 3. Struck out—By Schumacher 7, Bowman 1, Lanning 2. Hits—Off Bowman 5 in 4 innings (none out in fifth), Lanahan 4 in 1-3, Lanning 8 in 3 2-3. Hit by pitcher—By Bowman (Schumacher, Moore). Losing pitcher—Bowman. Umpires—Ballanfant, Campbell and Klem. Time of game—2:22. Attendance—5,941.

had 3 hits in a World Series game.

For 3 years (1938-40), Harry batted over .300, and in 1940 finished the season with 91 RBI.

During his time with the Giants, he also had 5 hits in 1 game ('37), and had 3 hits and 3 RBI in the last game at Philadelphia's Baker Bowl ('38), was 1 of 5 Giants to homer in 1 inning ('39), and had a single, double, triple and a homer in 1 game ('40).

Throughout his major league days—all spent with the Giants—he wielded a bat with as much confidence as he showed behind the plate. In those 10 seasons, he had 847 hits in 890 games with a .285 batting average.

For his efforts, he was selected to the National League All-Star squad from '38-41.

Harry, a widower, served in the military ('43-'45), but could not resume his baseball career due to arthritic knees. He was in the insurance field until his retirement in 1976.

ɔnce-in-a-career record, on June 15, 0, *Harry Danning* stroked his bat for a ʒle, double, triple and a home run in ʒ game.

Harry is a member of the Sportsman's B'nai B'rith Lodge in Chicago and is a member of the Maccabee Hall of Fame at the Hebrew University in Jerusalem.

ANSWERS

253. ▶ *Sandy Koufax.*

254. ▶ *Harry Danning.* On October 9, 1937, in the fourth game, *Danning* had a second inning run-scoring single off Bump Hadley. Batting against Ivy Andrews, he singled in the third inning and had a run-scoring double in the seventh inning. Carl Hubbell yielded 6 hits, as the New York Giants defeated the New York Yankees, at the Polo Grounds, 7-3.

255. ▶ Dave Boswell. On July 16, 1971, in the seventh inning, the California Angels reliever hit a solo homer. Clyde Wright was the winning pitcher, as the Angels defeated the Baltimore Orioles, at Anaheim Stadium, 5-4. Mike Cuellar, who had won 11 consecutive games, took the loss.

256. ▶ *Goody Rosen.* On May 17, 1938, in the sixth inning with 2 out, the Brooklyn Dodgers left fielder singled to left field and scored when Joe Medwick misplayed the ball. The St. Louis Cardinals defeated the Dodgers, at Ebbets Field, 2-1. Luke Hamlin was the losing pitcher.

257. ▶ *Ed Reulbach.* On May 30, 1905, in the morning game, *Reulbach* yielded 5 hits, as the Chicago Cubs defeated the Cincinnati Reds, at Palace of the Fans (Redland Field), 1-0. Jack O'Neill caught the victory.

258. ▶ *Sammy Bohne.*

259. ► Stan Ferens surrendered this Jewish slugger's 306th and last American League home run . . . ?

260. ► In 1977, Bill Travers surrendered this Twins' 239th and last hit of the season . . . ?

261. ► This Jewish player (1957-1967) hurled 28 complete games, including 10 shutouts . . . ?

262. ► *Morrie Arnovich* hit his first career home run in this Bowl . . . ?

263. ► This hurler surrendered *Heinie Scheer's* first hit and five years later Babe Ruth's record-setting 60th homer . . . ?

264. ► This California Angels manager was a coach in the 1970 All-Star Game . . . ?

(Answers next page.)

ANSWERS

259. ► *Hank Greenberg.* On September 26, 1946, in the eighth inning, *Greenberg* hit his league-leading 44th home run. Earlier in the game, the Detroit Tigers slugger homered off Denny Galehouse. Lou Kretlow yielded 7 hits, as the Tigers defeated the St. Louis Browns, at Briggs Stadium, 6-3. Ferens was the losing pitcher.

260. ► *Rod Carew.* On October 2, 1977, the Minnesota Twins first baseman had 3 singles, scored 2 runs and drove in his 100th run of the season. Dave Goltz yielded 7 hits in winning his twentieth game. The Twins defeated the Milwaukee Brewers, at County Stadium, 6-2. *Carew* won his sixth batting title with a .388 average.

261. ► *Barry Latman,* who ended his career with a 59-68 record.

262. ► Baker Bowl, Philadelphia. On September 27, 1936, in the second game of a doubleheader, the Philadelphia Phillies left fielder homered off Ben Cantwell. Claude Passeau yielded 12 hits, as the Phillies defeated the Boston Braves, 4-3.

263. ► Tom Zachary. On June 25, 1922, in the ninth inning, *Scheer* batted for pitcher Slim Harriss and singled. Zachary yielded 6 hits, as the Washington Senators defeated the Philadelphia Athletics, at Griffith Stadium, 2-1. *Scheer* had 73 hits and a .212 career batting average (1922-1923).

264. ► *Lefty Phillips.*

HALL
OF
FAME
265. ► *Sandy Koufax'* twenty-seventh win clinched the pennant for the Dodgers on the last day of the 1966 season. The losing Phillies hurler had won more than 100 games in each league...?

ALL-STARS
266. ► *Cy Block* made his only World Series appearance in this Chicago stadium...?

1960-
PRESENT
267. ► Name 2 of the 3 Jewish players on the 1978 Chicago White Sox...?

1930-59
268. ► This Braves pitcher, known as "Bear Tracks," surrendered *Harry Feldman's* first career hit...?

OLD-TIMERS
1857-1929
269. ► In 1877, Amos Booth surrendered this Jewish outfielder's only major league hit...?

BASEBALL
MISCELLANY
270. ► Who is the Jewish singer of the National Anthem at Yankee Stadium?

(Answers next page.)

ANSWERS

265. ► Jim Bunning. On October 2, 1966, in the second game of a doubleheader, *Koufax* struck out 10 batters and yielded 7 hits in winning his last major league game. The Los Angeles Dodgers defeated the Philadelphia Phillies, at Connie Mack Stadium, 6-3.

266. ► Wrigley Field. On October 8, 1945, in the ninth inning of the sixth game, *Block* ran for Chicago Cubs pinch-hitter Heinz Becker. Hank Borowy was the winning pitcher, as the Cubs defeated the Detroit Tigers, in twelve innings, 8-7.

267. ► *Ross Baumgarten, Ron Blomberg* and *Steve Stone.*

268. ► Al Javery. On September 27, 1941, in the fifth inning, the New York Giants pitcher singled. The Boston Braves defeated the Giants, at Braves Field, 5-4.

269. ► *Jay Pike.* On August 27, 1877, the Hartfords of Brooklyn right fielder appeared in his only major league game and singled. Terry Larkin yielded 9 hits, as the Hartfords defeated the Cincinnati Reds, at Brooklyn's Union Grounds, 5-1. Jay's brother, *Lipman Pike,* had 1 hit and scored the Reds' only run.

270. ► *Robert Merrill.*

HALL
OF
FAME
271. ► This Cubs hurler, who had won 2 games in the 1945 World Series, surrendered *Hank Greenberg*'s first National League hit . . . ?

ALL-STARS
272. ► In 1938, *Goody Rosen* had 8 consecutive hits. This Cardinals rookie hurler, who later won the final game of the 1944 World Series, stopped the streak . . . ?

1960-
PRESENT
273. ► These Jewish brothers played for the Los Angeles Dodgers . . . ?

1930-59
274. ► He caught Bob Feller's opening day no-hitter and *Harry Eisenstat*'s only career shutout . . . ?

OLD-TIMERS
1857-1929
275. ► This 4-time 20-game winner, nicknamed "Brickyard," was the losing pitcher when *Herman Iburg* won his first major league game . . . ?

BASEBALL
MISCELLANY
276. ► Who is the Jewish author of the baseball-oriented book *Bo: Pitching and Wooing*?

(Answers next page.)

ANSWERS

271. ▶ Hank Borowy. On April 15, 1947, in the sixth inning on Opening Day, *Greenberg's* double scored Billy Cox. Rip Sewell was the winning pitcher, as the Pittsburgh Pirates defeated the Chicago Cubs, at Wrigley Field, 1-0.

ALL-STARS

272. ▶ Max Lanier. On May 10, 1938, in the fourth inning, *Rosen* grounded out to St. Louis Cardinals shortstop Jimmy Brown. Luke Hamlin yielded 7 hits, as the Brooklyn Dodgers defeated the Cardinals, at Sportsman's Park, 10-2. Si Johnson took the loss.

1960-
PRESENT

273. ▶ *Larry* and *Norm Sherry*.

1930-59

274. ▶ Rollie Hemsley. On August 25, 1939, *Eisenstat* yielded 6 hits, as the Cleveland Indians defeated the Philadelphia Athletics, at League Park, 6-0. Lynn Nelson was the losing pitcher.

OLD-TIMERS
1857-1929

275. ▶ Brickyard Kennedy. On April 18, 1902, in the Philadelphia Phillies' home opener, Iburg yielded 5 hits and struck out 8 batters. The Phillies defeated the New York Giants, at Philadelphia Ball Park, 9-2. Red Dooin caught the victory. In his only major league season, Iburg had 11 wins, 18 losses in 30 games and a 3.89 ERA.

BASEBALL
MISCELLANY

276. ▶ *Maury Allen*.

HALL
OF
FAME
277. ► In a 1960 game, Bennie Daniels' single was the only hit off this Dodgers hurler...?

ALL-STARS
278. ► Who was the Indians Jewish slugger who had more than 100 RBI for 5 consecutive years (1950-1954)?

1960-
PRESENT
279. ► In 1977, Doug Bird surrendered this Jewish catcher's first major league home run...?

1930-59
280. ► This member of the 1950 pennant-winning Phillies caught *Moe Savransky* in his major league debut...?

OLD-TIMERS
1857-1929
281. ► *Joseph Bennett* made his only major league appearance in this Philadelphia stadium...?

BASEBALL
MISCELLANY
282. ► Who was the first known Jewish baseball player?

127   (Answers next page.)

ANSWERS

277. ► *Sandy Koufax.* On May 23, 1960, in the second inning, the Pittsburgh Pirates pitcher singled. *Koufax* fanned 10 batters, as the Los Angeles Dodgers defeated the Pirates, at Forbes Field, 1-0.

278. ► *Al Rosen.* In his 10-season career he batted in 717 runs, and belted 192 home runs.

279. ► *Jeff Newman.* On July 10, 1977, in the ninth inning, the Oakland Athletics catcher hit a solo home run. The Kansas City Royals scored 3 runs in the ninth inning and defeated the Athletics, at Royals Stadium, 5-4. Dave Giusti took the loss.

280. ► Andy Seminick. On April 23, 1954, the Cincinnati Redlegs reliever hurled a scoreless ninth inning, allowing 1 hit. Bob Rush yielded 6 hits, as the Chicago Cubs defeated the Redlegs, at Crosley Field, 10-3. Fred Baczewski was the losing pitcher.

281. ► Baker Bowl. On July 5, 1923, the Philadelphia Phillies substitute third-baseman did not bat and had 1 assist. Lou North was the winning pitcher, as the St. Louis Cardinals defeated the Phillies, 16-12. Rogers Hornsby hit 2 homers.

282. ► *Boaz Pike* of Brooklyn, the older brother of *Lipman Pike*, played in 1857.

HALL
OF
FAME

283. ► In 1935, this Red Sox hurler won 25 games and surrendered *Hank Greenberg*'s league-leading thirty-sixth home run...?

ALL-STARS

284. ► In 1934, *Fred Sington* debuted and his first hit scored this Senators Jewish player...?

1960-
PRESENT

285. ► Name 2 of the 4 Jewish players on the 1967 Houston Astros?

1930-59

286. ► This White Sox 22-game winner and ERA leader gave up *Murray Franklin*'s first major league hit...?

OLD-TIMERS
1857-1929

287. ► In 1902, Tully Sparks allowed the first career hit to this Senators Jewish second baseman, who later became a successful minor league manager...?

BASEBALL
MISCELLANY

288. ► Who worked for the Chicago White Sox for over 40 years and in 1940 became the acting president upon the death of Louis Comiskey...?

ANSWERS

HALL
OF
FAME

283. ► Wes Ferrell. On September 17, 1935, in the third inning, *Greenberg's* homer scored Charlie Gehringer. Ferrell yielded 10 hits, as the Boston Red Sox defeated the Detroit Tigers, at Fenway Park, 5-4. Eldon Auker took the loss.

ALL-STARS

284. ► *Buddy Myer.* On September 23, 1934, in the first inning of the first game of a doubleheader, the Washington Senators right fielder had a run-scoring single off Merritt Cain. Monte Weaver yielded 8 hits, as the Senators defeated the Philadelphia Athletics, at Shibe Park, 2-1.

1960-
PRESENT

285. ► *Bo Belinsky, Barry Latman, Norm Miller* and *Larry Sherry.*

1930-59

286. ► Thornton Lee. On August 14, 1941, in the ninth inning of the first game of a doubleheader, *Franklin* batted for pitcher Tommy Bridges and doubled. But Lee showed his stuff as he kept the Detroit Tigers to 8 hits, as the Chicago White Sox defeated the Tigers, at Comiskey Park, 3-1.

OLD-TIMERS
1857-1929

287. ► *Jake Atz.* On September 24, 1902, the Washington Senators second baseman debuted, singled and scored 1 run. Al Orth yielded 5 hits, as the Senators defeated the Boston Somersets, at Washington's American League Park, 8-2.

BASEBALL
MISCELLANY

288. ► *Harry Grabiner.*

289. ► In 1963, this Hall of Famer set a record with 15 strikeouts in a World Series game...?

290. ► In 1925, this Yankee 4-time 20-game winner surrendered *Si Rosenthal's* first major league hit...?

291. ► This Twins second baseman stole home 7 times in 1969...?

292. ► Browns reliever *Sid Schacht* debuted in this stadium...?

293. ► This player, the oldest of 4 brothers to appear in the major leagues, caught *Ed Reulbach's* first career victory...?

294. ► Nicknamed "Lefty," this Jewish base-ball/basketball player appeared in one game for the 1929 Washington Senators...?

(Answers next page.)

ANSWERS

HALL
OF
FAME

289. ▶ *Sandy Koufax.* On October 2, 1963, the Los Angeles Dodgers hurler fanned pinch-hitter Harry Bright to end the first game of the Series. *Koufax* yielded 6 hits, as the Dodgers defeated the New York Yankees, at Yankee Stadium, 5-2. Previous record holder Carl Erskine of the Brooklyn Dodgers struck out 14 batters in a 1953 World Series game.

ALL-STARS

290. ▶ Bob Shawkey. On September 8, 1925, in the first game of a doubleheader, the Boston Red Sox left fielder debuted and singled. Shawkey, with relief help from Waite Hoyt, was the winning pitcher. The New York Yankees defeated the Red Sox, at Fenway Park, 5-4. Red Ruffing took the loss.

1960-
PRESENT

291. ▶ *Rod Carew.*

1930-59

292. ▶ Sportsman's Park, St. Louis. On April 23, 1950, in the second game of a doubleheader, Ray Boone's single off the St. Louis Browns rookie scored *Al Rosen* with the only run of the seventh inning. Steve Gromek was the winning pitcher, as the Cleveland Indians defeated the Browns, in a game called after 7 innings, 7-5. Ned Garver took the loss.

OLD-TIMERS
1857-1929

293. ▶ Jack O'Neill. On May 25, 1905, *Reulbach* relieved Carl Lundgren in the second inning and shut out the Philadelphia Phillies on 5 hits. The Chicago Cubs defeated the Phillies, at Philadelphia Ball Park (Baker Bowl), 9-4. *Reulbach* singled off Tully Sparks for his first hit.

BASEBALL
MISCELLANY

294. ▶ *Ed Wineapple.*

295. ► In 1947, Andy Hansen surrendered this Jewish slugger's eleventh and last career grand slam home run . . . ?

296. ► In 1972, this Royals Jewish outfielder batted .300 and played in the All-Star Game . . . ?

297. ► In 1973, Eddie Fisher surrendered this Tigers Jewish outfielder's first major league home run . . . ?

298. ► *Herb Karpel* debuted in this New York stadium . . . ?

299. ► This Giants hurler, the National League's 1912 ERA leader, surrendered *Sammy Bohne*'s first career hit . . . ?

300. ► Who is the Jewish author of *A Thinking Man's Guide to Baseball*?

(Answers on page 138.)

DESIRE WAS HIS GAME

"I had that burning desire the first day I stepped on the field at Yankee Stadium with my uncle, and we were able to walk around the infield after the ballgame. I stood at first base, looked up at the stands. I knew it was something I would spend years just daydreaming about. Putting my name on the dotted line was just the first step toward achieving that lifelong ambition," says *Mike Epstein.*

Mike is the second of three children of Jack and Evelyn Epstein. His father, a native of Toronto, Ontario, was a salesman, while his mother, a housewife, came from the Bronx, New York, where Mike was born on April 4, 1943.

The family settled in Los Angeles, California, where Mike attended Fairfax High School, graduating in 1961. There he played baseball and football. He enrolled at the University of California at Berkeley, graduating with a degree in Social Psychology in 1964.

He played college ball, batting .375, and then .384 in his senior year, when he was a Collegiate All-American.

Mike was on the first U.S. Olympic Baseball Team in Tokyo.

He signed a professional baseball contract with the Baltimore Orioles, reported to Stockton in 1965, led the California League in home runs and batting average (30 home runs, 100 RBI and a .338 average), and was named the Rookie of the Year and the Player of the Year.

In 1966, he performed for Rochester in the International League, won the home run and RBI titles (29 home runs, 102 RBI and a .309 average), was the Rookie and Player of the Year, and was selected by both Topps and *The Sporting News* as the Minor League Player of the Year.

This won him promotion to the Orioles at the end of the season; his first hit came at Anaheim Stadium where he singled and tripled, driving in three runs in the process.

Mike began the 1967 season with the Orioles, could not displace Boog Powell at first, and was assigned to Rochester. He refused to report, and was traded to the Washington Senators.

Mike recalls his first home run. "We opened in Yankee Stadium... I hit a home run that night (inside-the-park off Thad Tillotson). I knocked in another run...I remember the headlines in the *New York Daily News*: "Mick and Yanks 4, Epstein 2"

Following another year with the Senators (13 home runs and a .238 average), and a brief appearance with Buffalo in the International League, he played for pennant-winning LaGuaira Tiburones in the Venezuela Winter League (he returned to Venezuela in 1970).

In 1969, Mike had his most productive year in the majors, with 30 home runs, including 3 in 1 game, 5 runs-batted-in, and a .278 average.

He remained with the Senators until 1971, when he was traded to the Oakland Athletics, appearing in the Championship Series with them.

The following year, he had 26 home runs (Reggie Jackson had 5), including 4 consecutively, 70 RBI and a .270 average for the World Series champions.

In November, A's owner Charles Finley advised him of his trade for Horacio Pina to the Texas Rangers. "I was shocked," Mike recalls. "I led the A's in home runs. I had a lot of friends on the ballclub. And my wife was from Stockton."

He played for the Rangers (1973), before ending his career with the California Angels (1973-74).

"My challenge was to get to the big leagues. I was a Jewish kid who had bad elbows and bad eyes, and only *some* ability. I really had no reason being in the major leagues except for that sheer desire to get here."

In all or parts of 9 major league seasons, Mike appeared in 907 games, collecting 695 hits, including 130 home runs, and a .244 batting average.

In 9 seasons, *Mike Epstein* had 695 hits in 2,854 at bats, with 380 RBI, and 130 homers for a career .244 average.

During the off-seasons, Mike played twice in the Winter Leagues, and intermittently resided in Lusk, Wyoming, where he led the life of a cowboy, hunting and riding horses.

He now operates his own company dealing in precious metals, and resides in the Denver area with his wife, Barbara Gluskin, and their three children.

In commenting on his major league baseball career, Mike said: "I was representing my own people...I tried to be a gentleman. I really tried to provide a good image, and do the best I could to be a shining light for Jewish youth."

135

Mike Epstein takes a cut at ball in practice the day he hit a home run.

ANSWERS

HALL OF FAME

295. ► *Hank Greenberg*. On August 3, 1947, in the sixth inning of the first game of a doubleheader, the Pittsburgh Pirates first baseman hit his eighteenth homer of the season. Monte Kennedy was the winning pitcher, as the New York Giants defeated the Pirates, at Forbes Field, 11-8. Preacher Roe took the loss. In the second game, *Greenberg* hit solo home runs off Joe Beggs and Larry Jansen.

ALL-STARS

296. ► *Richie Scheinblum*.

1960-PRESENT

297. ► *Dick Sharon*. On May 31, 1973, in the fourth inning, the Detroit Tigers right fielder hit a solo home run. Fisher yielded 9 hits, as the Chicago White Sox defeated the Tigers, at White Sox Park, 10-2. Jim Perry was the losing pitcher.

1930-59

298. ► Yankee Stadium. On April 19, 1946, in the eighth inning on Opening Day at Yankee Stadium, *Karpel* relieved Joe Page with the bases loaded and retired Washington Senators right fielder Buddy Lewis on a pop-up to end the inning. The New York Yankees defeated the Senators, 7-6.

OLD-TIMERS 1857-1929

299. ► Jeff Tesreau. On September 23, 1916, in the eighth inning of the first game of a doubleheader, the St. Louis Cardinals shortstop singled. Tesreau yielded 6 hits, as the New York Giants defeated the Cardinals, at the Polo Grounds, 6-1. Milt Watson took the loss. This was the Giants' eighteenth consecutive victory. During the 1912 season Tesreau had a league-leading 1.96 ERA.

BASEBALL MISCELLANY

300. ► *Leonard Koppett*.

301. ► Braves pitcher Denny Lemaster surrendered *Sandy Koufax'* second and last major league home run at this stadium...?

302. ► In 1952, White Sox reliever Luis Aloma allowed this Jewish third baseman's league-leading 105th RBI...?

303. ► This Jewish hurler had 1,601 career strikeouts between 1965 and 1979...?

304. ► This Jewish first baseman hit the last home run by a member of the Philadelphia Athletics...?

305. ► This Chicago player was baseball's winningest pitcher (1890-1892) and later surrendered *Ike Samuels* first career hit...?

306. ► Born Reuben Cohen, he played briefly with the 1921 St. Louis Cardinals...?

    (Answers next page.)

ANSWERS

HALL
OF
FAME

301. ► County Stadium, Milwaukee. On July 20, 1963, in the fifth inning, *Koufax* hit a 3-run homer. Reliever Ron Perranoski was the winning pitcher, as the Los Angeles Dodgers defeated the Milwaukee Braves, 5-4. Claude Raymond took the loss.

ALL-STARS

302. ► *Al Rosen.* On September 24, 1952, in the seventh inning, the Cleveland Indians third baseman hit a 3-run homer. Bob Lemon yielded 3 hits, as the Indians defeated the Chicago White Sox, at Municipal Stadium, 6-0. Lou Kretlow was the losing pitcher.

1960-
PRESENT

303. ► *Ken Holtzman.*

1930-59

304. ► *Lou Limmer.* On September 25, 1954, in the seventh inning, the Philadelphia Athletics first baseman hit a solo home run off Johnny Sain. Allie Reynolds won his 182nd and last major league game, as the New York Yankees defeated the Athletics, at Yankee Stadium, 10-2. Bill Oster took the loss. The Athletics moved to Kansas City for the 1955 season.

OLD-TIMERS
1857-1929

305. ► Bill Hutchison. On August 3, 1895, *Samuels* replaced Tommy Dowd at third base and in his debut had 1 hit in 2 plate appearances. All told, Hutchison yielded 4 hits, as the Chicago Colts defeated the St. Louis Browns, at West Side Park, 6-0. Bill Kissinger was the losing pitcher. In this, his only season, *Samuels* had 17 hits and a .230 batting average.

BASEBALL
MISCELLANY

306. ► *Reuben Ewing.*

HALL
OF
FAME
307. ► This Phillies Hall of Famer surrendered *Cal Abrams'* first career hit...?

ALL-STARS
308. ► Ed Burns caught this Jewish hurler's twenty-first and last victory of the 1915 Phillies' pennant-winning season...?

1960-
PRESENT
309. ► This former Angels Cy Young Award winner surrendered *Elliott Maddox'* first major league hit...?

1930-59
310. ► Name 2 of the 4 Jewish players on the 1936 Washington Senators?

OLD-TIMERS
1857-1929
311. ► Pirates second baseman *Jake Pitler* made his major league debut in this stadium...?

BASEBALL
MISCELLANY
312. ► This Dayton, Ohio, sportswriter wrote a book called *The Main Spark*...?

(Answers next page.)

ANSWERS

307. ▶ Robin Roberts. On April 23, 1949, in the fourth inning, the Brooklyn Dodgers left fielder singled and scored. Erv Palica was the winning pitcher, as the Dodgers defeated the Philadelphia Phillies, at Shibe Park, 8-6.

308. ▶ *Erskine Mayer.* On October 6, 1915, in the first game of a doubleheader Burns was behind the plate when *Mayer* relieved Al Demaree and allowed 1 hit in 4 innings. The Philadelphia Phillies defeated the Brooklyn Dodgers, at Baker Bowl, 9-6. Duster Mails took the loss. During that game, *Mayer* hit his only home run of the season and Gavvy Cravath belted his league-leading twenty-fourth homer.

309. ▶ Dean Chance. On April 21, 1970, the Detroit Tigers third baseman had 2 singles and 1 RBI. Earl Wilson was the winning pitcher, as the Tigers defeated the Cleveland Indians, at Municipal Stadium, 5-3. Steve Hargan took the loss.

310. ▶ *Syd Cohen, Buddy Myer, Fred Sington* and *Chick Starr.*

311. ▶ Forbes Field, Pittsburgh. On May 30, 1917, in the morning game, *Pitler* singled, stole a base and scored 1 run. Reliever Phil Douglas was the winning pitcher, as the Chicago Cubs defeated the Pittsburgh Pirates, 6-5. Elmer Jacobs took the loss.

312. ▶ *Si Burick.*

HALL
OF
FAME

313. ▶ This player caught *Sandy Koufax'* 1963 no-hitter, the second of his career...?

ALL-STARS

314. ▶ In 1954, this baseball all-star, who also played professional basketball, surrendered *Moe Savransky's* only major league hit...?

1960-
PRESENT

315. ▶ In 1967, Thad Tillotson surrendered this Senators Jewish slugger's first major league home run...?

1930-59

316. ▶ In which stadium did the Cubs hurler *Ed Mayer* win his first major league game?

OLD-TIMERS
1857-1929

317. ▶ Name 2 of the 3 Jewish players that were in the Federal League?

BASEBALL
MISCELLANY

318. ▶ Early in the history of baseball, this Jewish professional ballplayer was a member of the Philadelphia Athletics and in 1866 hit 6 home runs in 1 game...?

ANSWERS

313. ► Johnny Roseboro. On May 11, 1963, *Koufax* allowed 2 walks and struck out 4 batters, as the Los Angeles Dodgers defeated the San Francisco Giants, at Dodger Stadium, 8-0. Juan Marichal was the losing pitcher.

ALL-STARS

314. ► Gene Conley. On July 11, 1954, in the third inning of the first game of a doubleheader, the Cincinnati Reds reliever singled and later scored. Consecutive seventh-inning home runs by Gus Bell and Ted Kluszewski gave the Reds the victory. Jackie Collum was the winning pitcher, as the Reds defeated the Milwaukee Braves, at Crosley Field, 6-5.

1960-
PRESENT

315. ► *Mike Epstein.* On June 5, 1967, in the fourth inning, Epstein's inside-the-park homer scored Bob Saverine. Tillotson yielded 6 hits, as the New York Yankees defeated the Washington Senators, at Yankee Stadium, 4-2. Mickey Mantle's eighth-inning homer off Darold Knowles was the winning run.

1930-59

316. ► Wrigley Field, Chicago. On April 19, 1958, in the eighth inning, home runs by Walt Moryn and Dale Long gave the Chicago Cubs relief pitcher a victory. The Cubs defeated the St. Louis Cardinals, 6-3. Larry Jackson took the loss.

OLD-TIMERS
1857-1929

317. ► *Benny Kauff,* outfielder who played in the Federal League with Indianapolis and Brooklyn, *Ed Reulbach,* pitcher with Newark, and *Mike Simon,* catcher with St. Louis, and Brooklyn.

BASEBALL
MISCELLANY

318. ► *Lipman Pike.*

319. ► Jewish player *Mike Simon* was the opposing catcher when this Hall of Famer won his 511th and last career victory...?

320. ► This White Sox Jewish hurler was the last pitcher to no-hit *Al Rosen*, who ended the 1953 season with a 20-game hitting streak...?

321. ► In 1969, Astros Jewish outfielder *Norm Miller* played in consecutive no-hitters hurled by these pitchers...?

322. ► *Lou Brower* made his major league debut in this Boston stadium...?

323. ► In 1915, Emil Huhn caught this Jewish hurler's fortieth and last career shutout...?

324. ► This Jewish newspaper columnist wrote "Baseball's Sad Lexicon," on the double play combination of Tinker to Evers to Chance...?

SCHEINBLUM BATS .308 IN JAPAN

Richie Scheinblum finished up the 1976 season with Japan's Hiroshima team in the Central League, batting .308.

"Only a few players had ever hit over .300 in the Central League," he said recently from his home in Southern California, where he resides with his wife Mary Almeida and their son Monte.

"I enjoyed my two years in Japan playing baseball for Hiroshima."

That included a .291 average the previous year for the pennant winners.

But '76 was his last year in a pro ball career that began 11 years before in Cleveland, and took him to Washington, Kansas City, Cincinnati, California, St. Louis *and* Japan.

A severed achilles tendon playing basketball ended his career.

Richie, the second of 5 children, was born November 5, 1942, in New York City. His father Fred, a native of New York, was a Certified Public Accountant, while his mother Lee came from Kamenets-Podolskiy in the Ukraine. Richie's mother died when he was seven, and his father remarried. He attended Dwight Morrow High School in Englewood, New Jersey, graduating in 1960. He was on the school's baseball team, initially as a second basemen. When he could not control his arm, he became an outfielder.

He played baseball at C.W. Post College before graduating with a degree in Business Administration in 1964.

Although he played for six major league teams with limited success, Richie swung a mean bat in the minors.

After signing a contract with the Cleveland Indians (and taking home a $12,000 bonus) in '64 ("Coming from Fort Apache in the Bronx, that was more money than my family and I had ever heard of," he recalled), he reported to Burlington in the Carolina League where he had a .309 batting average.

The following year he batted .318 on the roster of Salinas, in the California League.

Then .263 with Pawtucket in the Eastern League and .291 with Portland in the Pacific Coast League. Again with Portland, he had a .304 average. Richie saw limited duty with Cleveland in '65, '67-'68, before spending the entire '69 season with the Indians.

In '70 he was again in the minors, collecting 24 home runs and a .337 batting average with Wichita in the American Association.

The next year he became the American Association batting champion with a .388 average and 108 RBI for pennant-winning Denver,

Richie Scheinblum suits up for Cleveland Indians.

Richie's major league career did not equal the batting prowess he displayed with regularity in the minors, but he still had one .300 season in the American League.

This was during '72 while playing for the Royals. Not only did he bat .300, the sixth best in the league, he also played in the All-Star game in Atlanta.

In all, or parts of 8 Major League seasons, Richie appeared in 462 games, collecting 320 hits, with a .263 average.

Then came his 2 years in Japan.

Not bad for someone who was not highly regarded as a baseball player in his high school.

"They tried me out at second base, but I couldn't control my arm, nor could anyone else, so they threw me in the outfield.

"Then one day they gave me a bat..."

147

ANSWERS

319. ► Cy Young. On September 22, 1911, in the seventh inning, Jay Kirke doubled and later scored on Al Bridwell's single for the only run of the game. Young yielded 9 hits, including doubles by *Simon* and Bill McKechnie. The Boston Pilgrims defeated the Pittsburgh Pirates, at Forbes Field, 1-0. Babe Adams was the losing pitcher.

320. ► *Saul Rogovin.* On September 5, 1953, in the first game of a doubleheader, *Rosen,* the Cleveland Indians third baseman, had no hits in 4 at bats. *Rogovin* yielded 4 hits, as the Chicago White Sox defeated the Indians, at Municipal Stadium, 2-0. Early Wynn took the loss. During his hitting streak, *Rosen* had 31 hits, including 7 home runs and a .390 batting average.

321. ► Jim Maloney and Don Wilson.

322. ► Fenway Park. On June 13, 1931, the Detroit Tigers shortstop had no hits in 4 at bats. Ed Morris yielded 8 hits, as the Boston Red Sox defeated the Tigers, 7-1. Whit Wyatt was the losing pitcher. *Brower* had 10 hits and a .161 career batting average.

323. ► *Ed Reulbach.* On October 3, 1915, in the second game of a doubleheader on the last day of the Federal League's season, *Reulbach* yielded 3 hits and struck out 12 batters. The Newark Peppers defeated the Baltimore Terrapins, at Harrison Park, New Jersey, 6-0. Charlie Young took the loss.

324. ► *Franklin P Adams.*

HALL
OF
FAME

325. ► In 1940, Johnny Rigney yielded this Jewish Hall of Famer's league-leading 41st home run and 150th RBI . . . ?

ALL-STARS

326. ► This Dodgers first baseman hit the only ball which outfielder *Sid Gordon* misplayed during the 1952 season . . . ?

1960-
PRESENT

327. ► *Mike Epstein* had his first major league hit in this California stadium . . . ?

1930-59

328. ► This Phillies Jewish player had the last hit at Baker Bowl . . . ?

OLD-TIMERS
1857-1929

329. ► In 1923, this Athletics hurler, nicknamed "Slim," surrendered *Louis Rosenberg*'s only major league hit . . . ?

BASEBALL
MISCELLANY

330. ► This former Justice of the Supreme Court represented Curt Flood in his challenge against baseball's reserve system . . . ?

     (Answers next page.)

ANSWERS

325. ► *Hank Greenberg.* On September 25, 1940, in the seventh inning of the second game of a double-header, the Detroit Tigers slugger homered to tie the score. Bobo Newsom was the winning pitcher, as the Tigers defeated the Chicago White Sox, at Briggs Stadium, 3-2.

326. ► Gil Hodges. On April 16, 1952, in the third inning, the Boston Braves left fielder errored Hodges' wind-blown fly. All told, winning pitcher Chris Van Cuyk was aided by 7 Boston errors, as the Brooklyn Dodgers defeated the Braves, at Braves Field, 14-8. Max Surkont took the loss. In 1952, *Gordon* led National League outfielders with a .996 fielding average.

327. ► Anaheim Stadium. On September 24, 1966, the Baltimore Orioles first baseman had 2 hits, including a triple and 3 runs batted in. Wally Bunker was the winning pitcher, as the Orioles defeated the California Angels, 6-3. Clyde Wright took the loss.

328. ► *Phil Weintraub.*

329. ► Slim Harriss. On July 16, 1923, the Chicago White Sox second baseman singled. Harriss yielded 7 hits, as the Philadelphia Athletics defeated the White Sox, at Comiskey Park, 4-3. Ted Blankenship was the losing pitcher.

330. ► *Arthur Goldberg.*

HALL
OF
FAME

331. ► In 1905, *George Stone* was traded by the Boston Puritans to the St. Louis Browns for this Hall of Famer, a 3-time .400 hitter . . . ?

ALL-STARS

332. ► In the 1966 World Series, this Orioles catcher was the last player to bat against Hall of Famer *Sandy Koufax* . . . ?

1960-
PRESENT

333. ► This former Pirates batting champion singled for the only hit allowed by *Ken Holtzman* and Rollie Fingers in a 1973 game . . . ?

1930-59

334. ► In which New York stadium did *Harry Rosenberg* make his major league debut?

OLD-TIMERS
1857-1929

335. ► This 1960 San Francisco Giants manager surrendered *Sam Mayer*'s first major league hit . . . ?

BASEBALL
MISCELLANY

336. ► Who was the Jewish author of *Where Have You Gone, Joe DiMaggio?*

     (Answers next page.)

ANSWERS

331. ► Jessie Burkett.

332. ► Andy Etchebarren. On October 6, 1966, in the sixth inning of the second game, the Baltimore Orioles catcher hit into an inning-ending double play. Jim Palmer yielded 4 hits, as the Orioles defeated the Los Angeles Dodgers, at Dodger Stadium, 6-0.

333. ► Matty Alou. On May 31, 1973, with 2 out in the seventh inning, Alou ended *Holtzman's* perfect game with a single. In the eighth inning, Jim Hart's line drive was deflected by *Holtzman* to the first baseman for the out. Rollie Fingers relieved and allowed 1 walk, as the Oakland Athletics defeated the New York Yankees, at Yankee Stadium, 6-0. Mel Stottlemyre was the losing pitcher.

334. ► Polo Grounds. On July 15, 1930, in the second inning, Rosenberg batted for New York Giants reliever Joe Heving and walked. Ray Kolp was the winning pitcher, as the Cincinnati Reds defeated the Giants, 14-8. Carl Hubbell took the loss.

335. ► Tom Sheehan. On September 6, 1915, in the first game of a doubleheader, the Washington Senators right fielder singled. Doc Ayers yielded 9 hits, as the Senators defeated the Philadelphia Athletics, at Shibe Park, 5-3.

336. ► *Maury Allen.*

337. ► In a 1967 game, this Giants Hall of Famer surrendered Eddie Mathews 500th career home run and *Norm Miller*'s only homer of the season...?

338. ► In 1929, *Buddy Myer*'s 24-game hitting streak was stopped in which Washington stadium?

339. ► Name 2 of the 3 Jewish players on the 1971 Washington Senators...?

340. ► This hurler, who had 114 pinch-hits and a .281 career batting average, surrendered *Morrie Arnovich*'s first major league hit...?

341. ► In 1907, Gus Dorner allowed this Cubs Jewish hurler's only major league home run...?

342. ► Born Philip Cohen, this Jewish third baseman appeared in one game for the 1905 New York Highlanders...?

ANSWERS

337. ► Juan Marichal. On July 14, 1967, *Miller* hit a home run in the fourth inning and Mathews homered in the sixth inning for the Houston Astros. Dave Giusti, with relief help from *Larry Sherry*, was the winning pitcher. The Astros defeated the San Francisco Giants, at Candlestick Park, 8-6.

338. ► Griffith Stadium. On June 1, 1929, the Washington Senators third baseman's streak stopped when he had no hits in 3 at-bats. Lefty Stewart, winning pitcher Ed Strelecki and General Crowder surrendered 11 hits, as the St. Louis Browns defeated the Senators, 5-4. Firpo Marberry took the loss.

339. ► *Mike Epstein, Elliott Maddox* and *Richie Scheinblum.*

340. ► Red Lucas. On September 14, 1936, in the second game of a doubleheader at Baker Bowl, Philadelphia Phillies outfielder Arnovich debuted and replaced Johnny Moore in left field. He doubled and scored 1 run in 3 at-bats. However, Lucas' 10-hit game was enough, as the Pittsburgh Pirates defeated the Phillies in 10 innings, 6-5. Joe Bowman was the losing pitcher.

341. ► *Ed Reulbach.* On July 17, 1907, the Chicago Cubs pitcher homered. *Reulbach* yielded 8 hits, as the Cubs defeated the Boston Doves, at Boston's South End Grounds, 3-2.

342. ► *Phil Cooney.*

HALL
OF
FAME

343. ► In a 1959 game, *Sandy Koufax* fanned this former Phillies Rookie of the Year for his eighteenth strikeout....?

ALL-STARS

344. ► Who was the Twins star that became the 1967 Rookie of the Year?

1960-
PRESENT

345. ► In 1977, Jewish catcher *Jeff Newman* made his only major league appearance as a pitcher in this Kansas City Stadium...?

1930-59

346. ► In 1952, Vic Raschi hurled a 1-hitter, allowing only a home run to this Tigers Jewish catcher...?

OLD-TIMERS
1857-1929

347. ► In 1910, Cy Falkenberg surrendered this Jewish outfielder's 985th and last career hit...?

BASEBALL
MISCELLANY

348. ► Forbes Field was constructed during his ownership of the Pittsburgh Pirates...?

(Answers on page 158.)

THE MORNING SALUTE

Each morning, 87-year-old *Robert Berman* gets up in his apartment in New York City and faces a photograph of the 1918 Washington Senators.

"I always salute," he says.

Then his day begins.

"I am the sole survivor of that ball club," he reminds you.

In '18, during a season curtailed by World War I, Babe Ruth won his first home run title, legendary pitcher Walter Johnson won 23 games, and 19-year-old Robert Berman made his second of 2 appearances for the Senators.

He was sent in to catch Walter Johnson.

"Walter was my God in those days," he recalls.

"I was nervous, but he said, 'Bobby, just remember, we're down in the bullpen, that's all.'"

There were no more opportunities for the son of Russian immigrants to take the field. He spent much of that season as a third-string catcher behind Eddie Ainsmith and Pat Gharrity before being sent to Jersey City in the International League.

But that one year began a love affair with the Senators that continues through today.

In 1919, Robert was behind the plate for Jersey City and was reunited with Al Schacht whom he had known from P.S. 42. The next year Al became a Washington Senator and went on to become the Clown Prince of Baseball.

Robert first met Schacht when he moved with his family to the Bronx from "a cold water flat on the Lower East Side."

He was born January 24, 1899,

BERMAN CATCHES JOHNSON
Gather Six Runs in Final Frame, Beating Browns by 6 to 4.

WASHINGTON (A)	ab	r	h	a	ST. LOUIS (A)	ab	r	h	a
Shotton, rf	4	1	2	1	Tobin, cf	5	0	1	0
Judge, 1b	4	0	1	0	Maisel, 3b	4	0	0	2
Foster, 3b	5	1	2	0	Sisler, 1b	5	1	3	1
Milan, cf	4	1	2	0	Hendryx, rf	3	1	2	0
Shanks, lf	3	0	1	1	Smith, lf	4	0	0	0
Morgan, 2b	4	0	1	0	Gedeon, 2b	3	1	0	2
Lavan, ss	4	1	2	2	d)Demmitt	0	0	0	0
Picinich, c	3	0	0	2	Gerrber, ss	2	1	0	3
a)W. J'nson, p	1	1	1	0	e)C. Johnson	1	0	0	0
Harper, p	2	0	0	2	Severeid, c	4	0	2	0
b)Ainsmith	1	0	0	0	Shocker, p	4	0	2	4
Reese, p	0	0	0	0	Gallia, p	0	0	0	0
c)Schulte	1	1	1	0		—	—	—	—
Berman, c	0	0	0	0	Total	35	4	10	13
	—	—	—	—					
Total	36	6	13	11					

a)Batted for Picinich in ninth; b)Batted for Harper in eighth; c) Batted for Reese in ninth; d) Batted for Gedeon in ninth; e) Batted for Gerber in ninth.

Washington	0 0 0 0 0 0 0 6—6
St. Louis	0 2 1 0 0 0 1 0 0—4

Two base hit—Shanks, Shocker, Milan, W. Johnson, Shotton. Stolen bases—Sisler(2). Sacrifice flies—Smith, Shanks. Double plays—Shocker, Gedeon, and Sisler; Gerber, Gegeon, and Sisler (2); Shanks and Lavan; Shotton asnd Picinich. Left on bases—Washington, 8; St. Louis, 13. First base on error—St. Louis. Bases on balls—Off Harper, 5; Reese, 2; Shocker, 2; Gallis, 2; Johnson, 1; Hits—Off Harper, 8 in 7; Johnson, 1 in 1; Reese 1 in 1; Shocker, 12 in 8⅔; Gallia, 1 in ⅓. Struck out—By Harper, 1; Reese, 1; Johnson, 2; Shocker, 1; Gallia, 1. Wild pitch—Shocker. Passed ball—Picinich. Winning pitcher—Reese. Losing pitcher—Shocker.

Robert Berman suits up in the uniform of the 1918 Washington Senators.

in New York City to Morris and Lena who a few years earlier had been part of the greatest wave of Jewish immigrants from Russia to the United States.

He attended Townsend Harris Hall, and finally Evander Childs High School, graduating in 1916.

While he was at Evander Childs, Robert was a catcher.

"In those days," he recalls, "the high school ballplayers were much older as players than they are today. We had boys on the club [high school] who were nineteen and twenty years of age."

From high school Robert enrolled in the City College of New York, and 2 years later signed with the Senators.

Robert was in professional baseball for 5 years, also playing for Binghamton and Syracuse, New York.

That was the end of his full-time career, but with college completed —he graduated from Savage School of Physical Education in '25—during the summers he put on his face mask and glove for the semi-pro South Philadelphia Hebrews, a team organized by Eddie Gottlieb of basketball fame.

Other summers he played for The Bushwicks and The Farmers in the New York area.

For 43 years he was a health education teacher, baseball coach, and/or Dean of Boys for the New York City Board of Education.

From '37 until he retired in '68, he taught at Franklin K. Lane High School, Brooklyn, New York.

He was married to dance instructor Dorothy Schramps in '26 (passed away, '76) and then to Lucille (passed away, '84). His daughter Barbara lives in Connecticut.

ANSWERS

343. ► Jack Sanford. On August 31, 1959, in the ninth inning, *Koufax* fanned Eddie Bressoud, Danny O'Connell and Sanford in succession. In the bottom of the ninth inning, Wally Moon's homer scored *Koufax* and Jim Gilliam. The Los Angeles Dodgers defeated the San Francisco Giants, at the Los Angeles Memorial Coliseum, 5-2. In his previous game, *Koufax* had 16 strikeouts.

344. ► *Rod Carew.*

345. ► Royals Stadium. On September 14, 1977, in the eighth inning of the second game of a twi-night doubleheader, Tim Hosley replaced *Newman* as the Oakland Athletics catcher. Newman hurled a scoreless inning, allowed 1 hit and hit a batter with a pitch. Dennis Leonard yielded 8 hits, as the Kansas City Royals defeated the Athletics, 6-0. Matt Keough took the loss.

346. ► *Joe Ginsberg.* On July 13, 1952, in the eighth inning with 2 out, the Detroit Tigers catcher belted a long homer. However, Raschi won the 100th game of his career, as the New York Yankees defeated the Tigers, at Yankee Stadium, 11-1. Art Houtteman was the losing pitcher. Home runs were also hit by Joe Collins, Yogi Berra and Mickey Mantle.

347. ► *George Stone.* On October 9, 1910, in the second game of a doubleheader, the St. Louis Browns left fielder had 1 hit in 4 plate appearances. Falkenberg yielded 5 hits, as the Cleveland Naps defeated the Browns, at Sportsman's Park, 3-0. Alex Malloy took the loss. *Stone* had a .301 career batting average.

348. ► *Barney Dreyfuss.*

349. ▶ This Cubs hurler (1926-1941) surrendered *Hank Greenberg*'s only 1935 World Series hit ...?

350. ▶ In 1958, which 3-time Phillies All-Star surrendered *Don Taussig*'s first major league hit?

351. ▶ Name 2 of the 3 Jewish players on the 1973 California Angels ...?

352. ▶ Bud Sheely caught this American League ERA leader's last game of the 1951 season ...?

353. ▶ Jewish Batting Champion *Benny Kauff* made his last appearance in the Federal League in this Brooklyn stadium ...?

354. ▶ This Jewish author wrote *The Baseball Book of Why* ...?

      (Answers next page.)

ANSWERS

349. ▶ Charlie Root. On October 3, 1935, in the first inning of the second game, *Greenberg*'s homer scored Charlie Gehringer. Tommy Bridges yielded 6 hits, as the Detroit Tigers defeated the Chicago Cubs, at Navin Field, 8-3. *Greenberg* was hit by a pitch in the seventh inning, sustained a broken wrist and did not appear in the remaining games of that World Series.

350. ▶ Curt Simmons. On April 29, 1958, the San Francisco Giants right fielder had 2 singles in 3 at bats. Simmons, with relief help from Dick Farrell, was the winning pitcher, as the Philadelphia Phillies defeated the Giants, at Seals Stadium, 7-4. Ray Monzant took the loss. *Taussig* had 69 hits and a .262 career batting average.

351. ▶ *Lloyd Allen, Mike Epstein* and *Richie Scheinblum.*

352. ▶ *Saul Rogovin.* On September 20, 1951, Joe Collins' eighth-inning homer scored Phil Rizzuto and Mickey Mantle to give *Rogovin* his eighth defeat in 20 decisions. Reliever Bobby Hogue was the winning pitcher, as the New York Yankees defeated the Chicago White Sox, at Yankee Stadium, 5-4. *Rogovin* hurled for the Tigers and White Sox and posted a league-leading 2.78 ERA.

353. ▶ Washington Park. On September 30, 1915, the Brooklyn Tip Tops center fielder had 2 hits, including a double. Gene Krapp yielded 6 hits, as the Buffalo Blues defeated the Tip Tops, 3-2. Don Marion was the losing pitcher.

354. ▶ *Dan Schlossberg.*

HALL
OF
FAME

355. ► This Dodger caught *Sandy Koufax'* fortieth and last career shutout . . . ?

ALL-STARS

356. ► This Cubs Jewish hurler was the first pitcher to strike out Hall of Famer Ty Cobb in a World Series game . . . ?

1960-
PRESENT

357. ► In 1960, *Barry Latman* was traded by the Chicago White Sox to the Cleveland Indians for this pitcher, whose career was shattered by a baseball . . . ?

1930-59

358. ► In 1953, the Braves transferred from Boston to Milwaukee. Who was the Jewish outfielder that had the team's first RBI of the season . . . ?

OLD-TIMERS
1857-1929

359. ► In 1888, *Julie Freeman* appeared in his only major league game for this American Association pennant-winning team, managed by Charlie Comiskey . . . ?

BASEBALL
MISCELLANY

360. ► This St. Louis Browns Jewish outfielder was the first batter at White Sox (Comiskey) Park . . . ?

      (Answers next page.)

ANSWERS

355. ▶ Johnny Roseboro. On September 11, 1966, in the first game of a doubleheader, *Koufax* yielded 6 hits, as the Los Angeles Dodgers defeated the Houston Astros, at Dodger Stadium, 4-0. Larry Dierker was the losing pitcher.

356. ▶ *Ed Reulbach.* On October 10, 1907, in the second inning of the third game, Cobb fanned. *Reulbach* yielded 6 hits, as the Chicago Cubs defeated the Detroit Tigers, at West Side Park, 5-1. Ed Siever took the loss.

357. ▶ Herb Score. In a 1957 game he was hit in the face by a batted ball.

358. ▶ *Sid Gordon.* On April 13, 1953, in the first inning, Bill Bruton singled, stole second and scored on *Gordon's* single. Max Surkont yielded 3 hits, as the Milwaukee Braves defeated the Cincinnati Redlegs, on opening day at Crosley Field, 2-0. Bud Podbielan was the losing pitcher.

359. ▶ St. Louis Browns. On October 10, 1888, the St. Louis Browns pitcher lost his only decision. Late in the game, *Freeman* broke his finger on a ball hit by Dude Esterbrook. Toad Ramsey yielded 5 hits, as the Louisville Colonels defeated the Browns, 7-4. *Freeman* had 1 hit and a .333 batting average.

360. ▶ *George Stone.*

361. ► During the 1939 season, *Harry Eisenstat* was traded by the Detroit Tigers to the Cleveland Indians for this Hall of Famer from Snohomish, Washington...?

362. ► In 1935, Earl Caldwell allowed this Jewish slugger's 200th hit of the season...?

363. ► This Brewers catcher homered for the only hit allowed by *Steve Stone* and Tippy Martinez in a 1979 game...?

364. ► Catcher *Chick Starr* appeared in 13 major league games(1935-1936) and caught only 1 complete-game victory. Who was the winning Senators pitcher who also hurled a shutout in the 1933 World Series?

365. ► Athletics Jewish infielder *Heine Scheer* belted his first major league home run in this stadium...?

366. ► Who was the Jewish catcher that appeared in 1 game with the 1937 Cincinnati Reds and later hit safely in 49 consecutive minor league games?

(Answers next page.)

ANSWERS

361. ▶ Earl Averill.

362. ▶ *Hank Greenberg.* On September 22, 1935, *Greenberg* doubled and achieved the 200-hit total for the second consecutive year. Caldwell yielded 3 hits, as the St. Louis Browns defeated the Detroit Tigers, at Navin Field, 1-0. Schoolboy Rowe was the losing pitcher.

363. ▶ Charlie Moore. On July 30, 1979, in the third inning, Moore homered. *Stone* was relieved in the ninth inning by Martinez who retired the last batter. The Baltimore Orioles defeated the Milwaukee Brewers, at County Stadium, 2-1. Jim Slaton took the loss.

364. ▶ Earl Whitehill. On September 2, 1935, in the second game of a doubleheader, *Starr*, the Washington Senators catcher, had 1 hit in 6 plate appearances. In the thirteenth inning, *Buddy Myer* singled and scored on Red Kress' base hit. Whitehill yielded 10 hits, as the Senators defeated the Boston Red Sox, at Fenway Park, 3-2. Gordon Rhodes was the losing pitcher.

365. ▶ Shibe Park, Philadelphia. On August 28, 1922, in the second inning of the second game of a doubleheader, the Philadelphia Athletics third baseman hit a 2-run homer off Frank Mack. Rollie Naylor yielded 11 hits, as the Athletics defeated the Chicago White Sox, 7-2. *Scheer* had 6 career home runs (1922-1923).

366. ▶ *Harry Chozen.*

HALL
OF
FAME
367. ► Who was the second string player that caught *Sandy Koufax'* third career no-hitter?

ALL-STARS
368. ► Nicknamed "The Barber," this pitcher surrendered *Al Rosen*'s first World Series hit...?

1960-
PRESENT
369. ► Mike Corkins surrendered the last career hit to this Jewish outfielder, a member of the 1969 New York Mets...?

1930-59
370. ► Twice during the 1944 season, this Giants Jewish first baseman scored 5 runs in a game...?

OLD-TIMERS
1857-1929
371. ► *Benny Kauff* made his major league debut in this Boston stadium...?

BASEBALL
MISCELLANY
372. ► Who was the author of *The Jew in American Sports*?

ROSEN MANAGES HIS OWN RETIREMENT

Al Rosen, a slugging third baseman for the Cleveland Indians, played more than 1,000 major league games. A minor league star, a major league MVP, he has proudly served baseball both as a player and an executive.

Al is one of two children born to Louis and Rose Rosen. His father's family came from Russia and settled in Macon, Georgia, while his mother's family arrived from Warsaw, Poland, and settled in Spartanburg, South Carolina, where Al was born on February 29, 1924. His parents were divorced when Al was very young, and he was raised in Miami, Florida, by his mother and grandmother. He received an athletic scholarship to the Florida Military Academy in St. Petersburg, graduating in 1941. There he played baseball and other sports.

Al enrolled at the University of Florida at Gainsville for one year, before playing with Thomasville in the North Carolina State League in 1942. Al says, "I was a walk-on with Thomasville.... I wanted to play baseball.... I showed up one day and signed a contract for ninety dollars a month." He batted .307 for the season. In September, he enrolled in an officer's candidate program at the University of Miami (graduating with a degree in Business Administration during the off-season in 1947), and en-

listed in the U.S. Navy, serving in the Pacific.

He joined the Cleveland Indians after his military discharge in 1946, and was assigned to Pittsfield, Massachusetts, in the Canadian-American League, where he was named the Most Valuable Rookie. In 1947, as the Oklahoma City third baseman, Al was the Texas League's Most Valuable Player, finishing with a league-leading .349 batting average and 141 runs batted in. He was promoted to the Indians at the end of the season, and had a pinch-hit single off Stubby Overmire, at Briggs Stadium, for his first major league hit.

Al began the 1948 season with the Indians, and was then sent to Kansas City, Missouri, in the American Association, where he hit five consecutive home runs, batted .327, and was the Rookie of the Year. He was recalled to the majors and appeared as a pinch-hitter in the World Series. He split the 1949 season between the Indians and San Diego in the Pacific Coast League before joining Cleveland in 1950, where he remained for the rest of his major league career.

Al has played in four All-Star Games (1952-55); two World Series (1948 and 1954); twice led the league in home runs (1950 and 1953); five times had one-hundred

Al Rosen has seen service as a player, over 1,000 games, two World Series, and as an executive with the Yankees and the Astros. Currently he is president and general manager of the San Francisco Giants.

or more runs batted in (1950-54), including two league-leading seasons (1952-53); and three times batted over .300 (1952-54). In 1953, he was a unanimous choice as the American League's Most Valuable Player. Al appeared in 1,044 major league games, with 1,063 hits, including 192 home runs, 717 RBI and a .285 batting average.

Al retired after the 1956 season, and was a stock broker before his association with Caesars Palace in Las Vegas, Nevada. He has been an executive with the New York Yankees and the Houston Astros, and now is President and General Manager of the San Francisco Giants. Al, a widower, is married to Rita Kallman. They have five children and one grandchild.

In 1980, Al was inducted into the Jewish Sports Hall of Fame in Israel. He is also a member of the Sports Hall of Fame located in Florida, Ohio and South Carolina. Al says, "I was very happy to be a professional baseball player, because it was somethig I always wanted to do."

ANSWERS

367. ► Doug Camilli. On June 4, 1964, *Koufax* fanned 12 batters and allowed only a fourth inning walk to Richie Allen. The Los Angeles Dodgers defeated the Philadelphia Phillies, at Connie Mack Stadium, 3-0. Chris Short was the losing pitcher. Frank Howard hit a 3-run homer.

368. ► Sal Maglie. On September 29, 1954, in the eighth inning of the first game, the Cleveland Indians third baseman singled. Don Liddle relieved Maglie and Vic Wertz then hit a long fly which Willie Mays caught near the center field bleachers. Dusty Rhodes' 3-run, pinch-hit homer in the tenth inning ended the game. Marv Grissom was the winning pitcher, as the New York Giants defeated the Indians, at the Polo Grounds, 5-2. Bob Lemon took the loss.

369. ► *Art Shamsky.* On June 13, 1972, in the ninth inning, *Shamsky* batted for Dan McGinn and singled off the San Diego Padres reliever. Clay Kirby was the winning pitcher, as the Padres defeated the Chicago Cubs, at Wrigley Field, 4-3. Milt Pappas took the loss. *Shamsky* had 426 hits and a .253 batting average.

370. ► *Phil Weintraub.*

371. ► Fenway Park. On April 20, 1912, at the opening of Fenway Park, *Kauff* was a late-inning replacement in center field for the New York Yankees. He had no hits and scored 1 run. Charley Hall was the winning pitcher, as the Boston Red Sox defeated the Yankees, in eleven innings, 7-6. Hippo Vaughn was the losing pitcher.

372. ► *Harold U. Ribalow.*

HALL
OF
FAME

373. ▶ Which Phillies Hall of Famer gave up 5 hits in a 1952 game to *Sid Gordon*?

ALL-STARS

374. ▶ In 1957, this White Sox All-Star caught pitcher *Barry Latman*'s first major league victory...?

1960-
PRESENT

375. ▶ In 1978, the Baltimore Orioles signed this future Cy Young Award winner as a free agent...?

1930-59

376. ▶ Slick Castleman was the winning pitcher of the last major league game at Philadelphia's Baker Bowl. This Jewish Giant caught the victory...?

OLD-TIMERS
1857-1929

377. ▶ Jimmy Archer was behind the plate for which Jewish hurler's fourteenth consecutive victory of the 1909 season?

BASEBALL
MISCELLANY

378. ▶ Who was the Jewish player on the Brooklyn Atlantics, the team that stopped the Cincinnati Red Stockings' 130-game winning streak in 1870?

     (Answers next page.)

ANSWERS

373. ▶ Robin Roberts. On September 6, 1952, in the first game of a doubleheader, the Boston Braves left fielder had 5 singles in 7 at-bats, scored 1 run and had 1 RBI. Del Ennis' seventeenth-inning homer won the game. Roberts yielded 18 hits in winning his twenty-third game. The Philadelphia Phillies defeated the Braves, at Shibe Park, 7-6. Bob Chipman took the loss.

ALL-STARS

374. ▶ Sherm Lollar. On September 15, 1957, *Latman* relieved Bob Keegan and hurled 2 scoreless innings. The Chicago White Sox scored 3 runs in the ninth inning and defeated the Washington Senators, at Griffith Stadium, 3-1. Tex Clevenger was the losing pitcher.

1960-
PRESENT

375. ▶ *Steve Stone.*

1930-59

376. ▶ *Harry Danning.* On June 30, 1938, the New York Giants catcher had 3 hits and 3 runs batted in. Castleman yielded 7 hits, including *Phil Weintraub*'s single, the last hit at Baker Bowl. The Giants defeated the Philadelphia Phillies, 14-1. Claude Passeau took the loss. The Phillies moved to Shibe Park.

OLD-TIMERS
1857-1929

377. ▶ *Ed Reulbach.* On August 10, 1909, *Reulbach* yielded 6 hits, as the Chicago Cubs defeated the Brooklyn Superbas, at West Side Park, 8-1. Jim Pastorius was the losing pitcher. *Reulbach* lost his next game on August 14th, as Red Ames and the New York Giants defeated the Cubs, 5-2.

BASEBALL
MISCELLANY

378. ▶ *Lipman Pike.*

HALL
OF
FAME
379. ▶ In 1922, *Heine Scheer* debuted against this Hall of Famer, who won 241 games...?

ALL-STARS
380. ▶ This Jewish catcher hit the last home run at the Los Angeles Memorial Coliseum...?

1960-
PRESENT
381. ▶ In 1961, *Howie Koplitz* won his first major league victory in this Los Angeles stadium...?

1930-59
382. ▶ Name 2 of the 3 Jewish players on the 1938 Philadelphia Phillies...?

OLD-TIMERS
1857-1929
383. ▶ In an 1884 Union Association game, Charlie Gagus of the Washington Nationals surrendered this Milwaukee Jewish outfielder's first career hit...?

BASEBALL
MISCELLANY
384. ▶ Who was the Jewish president of the 1982 pennant-winning Milwaukee Brewers?

ANSWERS

379. ▶ Herb Pennock. On April 20, 1922, in the third inning, *Scheer* batted for pitcher Eddie Rommel and was retired by the Boston Red Sox hurler. Pennock yielded 9 hits, as the Red Sox defeated the Philadelphia Athletics, at Shibe Park, 15-4.

ALL-STARS

380. ▶ *Norm Sherry.* On September 20, 1961, in the eighth inning of the final game at the Coliseum, the Los Angeles Dodgers catcher homered off Dick Ellsworth. *Sandy Koufax* yielded 7 hits and had 15 strikeouts, as the Dodgers defeated the Chicago Cubs, in 13 innings, 3-2. Barney Schultz was the losing pitcher. The Coliseum was the home of the Dodgers, 1958-1961.

1960-
PRESENT

381. ▶ Wrigley Field. On September 24, 1961, the Detroit Tigers reliever hurled 2 scoreless innings for a win as the Tigers defeated the Los Angeles Angels, in 10 innings, 7-5. Art Fowler took the loss.

1930-59

382. ▶ *Morrie Arnovich, Eddie Feinberg* and *Phil Weintraub.*

OLD-TIMERS
1857-1929

383. ▶ *Steve Behel.* On September 29, 1884, the left fielder had 1 hit in 4 plate appearances. Henry Porter was the winning pitcher, as Milwaukee defeated Washington, 7-5.

BASEBALL
MISCELLANY

384. ▶ *Bud Selig.*

HALL
OF
FAME
385. ► This Jewish slugger holds the Detroit Tigers all-time record for most RBIs in one season...?

ALL-STARS
386. ► Pitcher *Larry Sherry* won the first 1959 National League playoff game in this stadium...?

1960-PRESENT
387. ► In 1965, this Cubs Jewish hurler debuted and yielded a home run to Jim Hart...?

1930-59
388. ► Bob Weiland surrendered this Jewish scholar's first career home run...?

OLD-TIMERS
1857-1929
389. ► In 1929, Clise Dudley allowed this Jewish second baseman's 249th and last major league hit...?

BASEBALL
MISCELLANY
390. ► This Jewish announcer and Ed Fitzgerald wrote the book *You Can't Beat the Hours*...?

ANSWERS

385. ▶ *Hank Greenberg* had 183 RBI in 1937.

386. ▶ County Stadium, Milwaukee. On September 28, 1959, *Sherry* relieved Danny McDevitt and shut out the Milwaukee Braves on 4 hits in 7⅔ innings. The Los Angeles Dodgers defeated the Braves, 3-2. Carl Willey was the losing pitcher.

387. ▶ *Ken Holtzman.* On September 4, 1965, in the ninth inning, the Chicago Cubs reliever allowed a home run and then retired the remaining 3 batters. But Ron Herbel was the winning pitcher, as the San Francisco Giants defeated the Cubs, at Wrigley Field, 7-3. Bob Buhl took the loss.

388. ▶ *Moe Berg.* On April 23, 1932, in the seventh inning, the Washington Senators catcher homered. Carl Fischer yielded 4 hits, as the Senators defeated the Boston Red Sox, at Griffith Stadium, 5-0.

389. ▶ *Andy Cohen.* On September 28, 1929, in the second game of a doubleheader, the New York Giants second baseman singled. Dudley yielded 10 hits, as the Brooklyn Robins defeated the Giants, at the Polo Grounds, 10-3. Carl Hubbell was the losing pitcher. *Cohen* had a .281 career batting average.

390. ▶ *Mel Allen.*

HALL
OF
FAME
391. ► Moe Morhardt became the eighteenth strikeout of a 1962 game for this Jewish Hall of Famer...?

ALL-STARS
392. ► This Twins star was the American League's 1977 Most Valuable Player...?

1960-
PRESENT
393. ► This Mets Jewish outfielder was the last out of Bob Moose's 1969 no-hitter...?

1930-59
394. ► *Eddie Turchin*'s first major league hit was in this St. Louis stadium...?

OLD-TIMERS
1857-1929
395. ► In 1907, Ed Siever surrendered this Jewish hurler's only World Series hit...?

BASEBALL
MISCELLANY
396. ► This member of the College Football Hall of Fame was an outfielder with the Washington Senators and Brooklyn Dodgers (1934-1939)...?

A WINNING CURVE BALL

"I had a curve ball that fell off the table," recalls left-handed pitcher *Marv Rotblatt.*

"I never threw real hard, but I have led two or three leagues in strikeouts."

It was a curve ball that gave him many winning seasons.

Marv, born October 18, 1927, in Chicago, Illinois, the son of Sol, from Warsaw, Poland, and Carolyn attended Von Steuben High School.

By the time he had graduated from the University of Illinois with a Bachelor's degree in Journalism, that curve ball had helped him compile a 28-4 record, and enabled him to fan 18 batters in 1 game, and was 10-0 in a season. Both were Big Ten records.

His ability to fool the batter helped during Summer recess, '46-47, when he played for The House of David Baseball Club. The smallest player on the team, he was called 'Little David.' Playing against the Harlem Globetrotters (baseball team) this little David fanned 17.

"During my first year with The House of David, I won 14 in a row," he added.

This type of success attracted the attention of the professional baseball scouts. With graduation out of the way, in '48, the Chicago White Sox signed an interest in that curve ball. They gave him a

In 3 seasons, *Marv Rotblatt* appeared in 35 games.

chance to test it in the major leagues, putting him in relief against the Detroit Tigers at Comiskey Park.

"I was nervous," he said. "Kind of numb. I got the ball over the plate. Got 6 outs, including Dick Wakefield and Pat Mullin."

But 2 games later, he was hurling for Waterloo, Iowa, in the Three-I league.

With a record of 8 wins in 9 decisions in a 1-month stint that included 81 innings, 5 shutouts and a no-hitter, he was soon back with the White Sox.

He appeared in 5 games, starting 2.

Before he could make the major league rotation, he had to return to the minors, and hurled for Memphis in the Southern Association.

Then an injury to his arm took some of the curve out of his best pitch. He finished out the season with a record of 7-6.

In 1950, the injury appeared healed and the curve was back when he was 22-7 with Memphis. He also set a Southern Association record with 202 strikeouts, and led the league in innings pitched, complete games, and ERA.

This set of records gave Marv another shot in the major leagues. He appeared in 2 games with no decision.

The next season he won the second game of the season as a starter—then was sent to the bullpen.

"I am a starter, not a reliever," he says. "I didn't want to say anything. You didn't have agents in those days."

Agent or no agent, he appeared in 26 games (24 in relief), winning 4 of 6 decisions with a 3.40 ERA.

The curve was now established, but 2 years in the U.S. Army ('52-53) interrupted his career—and also ended it.

In the military he played on an interesting team with Bobby Brown, Hy Cohen, Don Newcombe, Gus Triandos and Bob Turley. He also injured his arm and became a 'junk-ball' pitcher.

Marv travelled the next 4 years, appearing with Charleston, South Carolina, in the American Association, Memphis ('54, where he had a 13-7 record), Atlanta, Monterey and Syracuse.

Another injury while compiling a 9-3 record for Syracuse ended his career in '57.

If the injuries had not occurred, Marv Rotblatt would probably have had an excellent major league career. As it was, he had a career of which he can be proud.

"I never had a losing year in my career at any level, anytime, anyplace," added the 5'6½" highly successful insurance executive.

MAYER BOWS TO MAYS

The Fall of 1957 is one San Francisco-born *Ed Mayer* can't forget, even as a man who chooses "not to live in the past."

That was the time he made it to the majors, and also gave up a home run to Willie Mays.

"He hit a ball over my head into the center field bleachers," he recalls.

That was in his major league debut at Wrigley Field.

"I also gave up 5 runs in 5 innings," he says.

"But I also got my first major league hit, a single off Giants pitcher Mike McCormick."

Born November 30, 1931, to a father who was a native of Hong Kong and a mother from Pennsylvania, he got his start in baseball via the University of California at Berkeley.

He left school in 1952 and signed a contract with the Boston Red Sox. He was later traded to

"If only Mays had whiffed," recalls *Ed Mayer.*

the St. Louis Cardinals who in turn traded him to the Chicago Cubs.

In his initial 5 years, Ed played for teams in Yuma, Arizona; San Jose, California; Greensboro, North Carolina; Montgomery, Alabama; and Omaha, Nebraska.

In '53 (his second year), he won 17 games for San Jose in the California League, and 17 again the next year for Greensboro in the Carolina League.

He was a good hitter, who sometimes played first base and in the outfield. During those early years in the minors, Ed was often on the All-Star team.

In the winter of '56 he went to Havana, Cuba, and badly injured his arm.

The next year he reported to Ft. Worth in the Texas League—a team shared by the Cubs *and* the Dodgers, and later that year was promoted to the majors where he met up for the first time with Willie Mays.

His strong record in the minors as a starter had earned him a spot in the majors as a reliever.

A baseball player does as he is told and has no rights," he says.

His first major league win came in April, 1958, when the Cubs beat the St. Louis Cardinals 6-3 on Ed's pitching and home runs by Walt Moryn and Dale Long.

All told, that season he won 2 of 4 games in 19 appearances.

He also appeared in 21 games with Portland in the Pacific Coast League.

His last 2 years were with Denver in the American Association *and* with Monterey in the Mexican League.

Not wanting to live in the past, when he threw the ball for the last time, Ed turned to education, graduating from UC at Berkeley with a teaching degree.

Ed has 3 children and 5 grandchildren. He lives with his second wife, Harriet, in the San Francisco area where he teaches fourth grade.

"Now, if only Mays had whiffed."

But, then, that would be living in the past!

JEW SITS IN CATHOLIC HALL OF FAME

Ed Wineapple had all the credentials to be inaugurated into the Providence College Hall of Fame. At the Catholic college he had made it on both the basketball and baseball All-America teams.

This had followed a stand-out year with Syracuse University where he was captain of the freshman baseball, football *and* basketball teams.

One hitch. Ed ain't Catholic, he's Jewish!

A multi-talented athlete who set many sports records at Salem High School in Massachusetts, actually his first love was football.

"I was going to give up baseball to go into professional football, but I hurt my leg badly in high school, then again in college," he recalls from New York where he retired and for twenty years was a representative for the Russ Togs Sportswear Company.

But the young man who was born August 10, 1906, in Boston, Massachusetts, to a father who owned a leather factory, had a bit of tough leather in him.

If he couldn't make it as a professional football player, he was determined to make it as a professional baseball player.

And he did, accepting a $5,000 offer from the Washington Senators in '29.

His debut at Griffith Stadium against the Detroit Tigers was

Ed Wineapple inaugurated into non-Jewish Providence College Hall of Fame.

unspectacular. He allowed 2 earned runs in 4 innings.

Because of his leg injury, Ed's baseball career was limited to 3 years,

He hurled for Chattanooga in the Southern League, Buffalo and Toronto in the International League, and Wilmington, North Carolina, in the Piedmont League.

During the winter months he played professional basketball with Syracuse.

When the administrators at Providence College decided to install a Hall of Fame, they also decided that Catholic or no, Ed belonged there. So much so that he was the first member of that illustrious body of athletes.

ANSWERS

391. ► *Sandy Koufax.* On April 24, 1962, in the ninth inning, Morhardt batted for Don Elston and fanned to end the game. *Koufax* gave up 6 hits, as the Los Angeles Dodgers defeated the Chicago Cubs, at Wrigley Field, 10-2. Don Cardwell was the losing pitcher.

ALL-STARS

392. ► *Rod Carew.*

1960-
PRESENT

393. ► *Art Shamsky.* On September 20, 1969, the New York Mets left fielder grounded to the second baseman for the final out. Moose allowed 3 walks and had 6 strikeouts, as the Pittsburgh Pirates defeated the Mets, at Shea Stadium, 4-0. Gary Gentry took the loss.

1930-59

394. ► Sportsman's Park. On May 9, 1943, in the ninth inning of the first game of a doubleheader, *Turchin* replaced Rusty Peters at shortstop for the Cleveland Indians. *Turchin* had 2 singles off Fritz Ostermueller, including a thirteenth-inning hit which scored pitcher Mike Naymick with the winning run. The Indians defeated the St. Louis Browns, 6-5. *Turchin* appeared in 11 games and had 3 hits, 1 RBI and a .231 career batting average.

OLD-TIMERS
1857-1929

395. ► *Ed Reulbach.* On October 10, 1907, in the fourth inning of the third game, the Chicago Cubs pitcher singled to score Joe Tinker. *Reulbach* yielded 6 hits, as the Cubs defeated the Detroit Tigers, at West Side Park, 5-1. *Johnny Kling* caught the victory.

BASEBALL
MISCELLANY

396. ► *Fred Sington.*

HALL
OF
FAME
397. ► In 1938, *Hank Greenberg* scored his league-leading 144th run in this Cleveland stadium . . . ?

ALL-STARS
398. ► In 1949, Lou Brissie allowed this Jewish third baseman's only All-Star Game hit . . . ?

1960-
PRESENT
399. ► This Jewish first baseman had 130 career home runs between 1966 and 1974...?

1930-59
400. ► In 1951, Jim Blackburn surrendered this Dodgers Jewish outfielder's first major league home run . . . ?

OLD-TIMERS
1857-1929
401. ► *Billy Nash* debuted against this 3-time, 30-game winner (1883-1885) for the Philadelphia Athletics of the American Association . . . ?

BASEBALL
MISCELLANY
402. ► This Cubs Jewish catcher was a holdout in 1909 when he became the Pocket Billiards Champion . . . ?

(Answers next page.)

ANSWERS

397. ► Municipal Stadium. On October 2, 1938, in the second game of a doubleheader, the Detroit Tigers first baseman had 3 singles, 1 RBI and scored 3 runs. Bob Harris gave up 11 hits, as the Tigers defeated the Cleveland Indians, in a game called after 7 innings, 10-8. John Humphries was the losing pitcher. *Greenberg* scored 2 runs in the first game, won by the Tigers, 4-1.

398. ► *Sid Gordon.* On July 12, 1949, in the fifth inning, the New York Giants third baseman doubled. Virgil Trucks was the winning pitcher, as the American League defeated the National League, at Ebbets Field, 11-7. Don Newcombe took the loss.

399. ► *Mike Epstein.*

400. ► *Cal Abrams.* On May 5, 1951, in the seventh inning, the Brooklyn Dodgers leftfielder blasted a 2-run homer. Chris Van Cuyk was the winning pitcher, as the Dodgers defeated the Cincinnati Reds, at Ebbets Field, 12-8. Ken Raffensberger took the loss.

401. ► Bobby Mathews. On August 5, 1884, in an American Association game, the Richmond Virginias third baseman, *Nash,* had no hits in 4 plate appearances facing Mathews. The pitcher allowed only 5 hits, as the Philadelphia Athletics defeated the Virginias, in Richmond, 14-0. Ed Dugan was the losing pitcher. This was the Virginias' first game in the league.

402. ► *Johnny Kling.*

HALL
OF
FAME
403. ▶ This Hall of Famer, nicknamed "Satchel," was the losing pitcher when *Saul Rogovin* won his fourteenth and final victory of the 1952 season...?

ALL-STARS
404. ▶ In 1959, Bob Anderson surrendered this Jewish Dodger's first major league hit...?

1960-
PRESENT
405. ▶ *Jeff Newman* hit his only home run of the 1984 season in this Toronto stadium...?

1930-59
406. ▶ In 1933, Tommy Thomas surrendered this Indians Jewish outfielder's only major league home run...?

OLD-TIMERS
1857-1929
407. ▶ *Steve Behel* and *Joe Strauss* were the only known Jewish players to appear in this 1884 league...?

BASEBALL
MISCELLANY
408. ▶ Authors Louis Kaufman, Barbara Fitzgerald and Tom Sewell wrote a book about this Jewish baseball player titled ...*Athlete, Scholar, Spy*...?

(Answers next page.)

ANSWERS

403. ▶ Satchel Paige. On September 26, 1952, Rogovin yielded 2 hits in winning his fourteenth game, the highest victory total of his major league career. The Chicago White Sox defeated the St. Louis Browns, at Comiskey Park, 6-2.

ALL-STARS

404. ▶ *Larry Sherry.* On July 4, 1959, in the first game of a doubleheader, the Los Angeles Dodgers hurler singled. Anderson yielded 6 hits, as the Chicago Cubs defeated the Dodgers, at Wrigley Field, 2-1. The unfortunate *Sherry* allowed 4 hits and had 7 strikeouts in losing his first decision.

1960-
PRESENT

405. ▶ Exhibition Stadium. On June 17, 1984, the Boston Red Sox catcher homered off reliever Roy Lee Jackson. Jim Clancy was the winning pitcher, as the Toronto Blue Jays defeated the Red Sox, 5-3. Rich Gale took the loss.

1930-59

406. ▶ *Milt Galatzer.* On June 27, 1933, in the fifth inning, the Cleveland Indians right fielder homered. Sarge Connally was the winning pitcher, as the Indians defeated the Washington Senators, at Municipal Stadium, 7-6. Bill McAfee was the losing pitcher.

OLD-TIMERS
1857-1929

407. ▶ The Union Association. This rival to the National League and American Association folded after a disastrous season.

BASEBALL
MISCELLANY

408. ▶ *Moe Berg.*

HALL
OF
FAME

409. ▶ This Dodger caught *Sandy Koufax'* perfect game, the fourth no-hitter of his career . . . ?

ALL-STARS

410. ▶ This Indians Jewish first baseman had 5 RBI in the 1954 All-Star Game . . . ?

1960-
PRESENT

411. ▶ In 1976, Chris Chambliss scored on this Jewish Yankees player's only RBI in a Championship Series game . . . ?

1930-59

412. ▶ In 1937, Ted Kleinhans gave up this Dodgers Jewish outfielder's first career hit . . . ?

OLD-TIMERS
1857-1929

413. ▶ In a 1906 game, Homer Smoot's single was the only hit allowed by this Cubs Jewish hurler . . . ?

BASEBALL
MISCELLANY

414. ▶ This Jewish shortstop played for the St. Louis Browns (1930-1933) and later became a professional football player with the Pittsburgh Pirates (1935-1936) . . . ?

     (Answers next page.)

ANSWERS

409. ▶ Jeff Torborg. On September 9, 1965, *Koufax* struck out 14 batters, as the Los Angeles Dodgers defeated the Chicago Cubs, at Dodger Stadium, 1-0. Cubs pitcher Bob Hendley allowed 1 hit, a seventh-inning double by Lou Johnson.

410. ▶ *Al Rosen.*

411. ▶ *Elliott Maddox.* On October 12, 1976, in the sixth inning of the third game, the New York Yankees right fielder had a run-scoring double off Steve Mingori. Dock Ellis, with relief help from Sparky Lyle, was the winning pitcher. The Yankees defeated the Kansas City Royals, at Yankee Stadium, 5-3. Andy Hassler took the loss.

412. ▶ *Goody Rosen.* On September 14, 1937, in the second game of a doubleheader, the Brooklyn Dodgers center fielder had 2 singles, 1 run-batted-in and a stolen base. Buck Marrow yielded 6 hits, as the Dodgers defeated the Cincinnati Reds, at Crosley Field, 11-2. Rosen debuted in the first game of the doubleheader as a pinch-runner.

413. ▶ *Ed Reulbach.* On June 25, 1906, *Reulbach* had 7 strikeouts and issued 3 walks, as the Chicago Cubs defeated the St. Louis Cardinals, at West Side Park, 2-1. John Thompson took the loss. In 1906, *Reulbach* won 20 games and led the league with an .833 pitching percentage.

414. ▶ *Jim Levey.*

415. ► In 1880, Jewish rookie *Dan Stearns* appeared in a no-hitter hurled by this Hall of Famer, nicknamed "Pud"...?

416. ► *Syd Cohen* lost his first game as a pitcher to which Indians All-Star hurler (1934-1937)?

417. ► This pitcher won 2 World Series games for the Milwaukee Brewers and in 1975 surrendered *Dick Sharon*'s last major league hit...?

418. ► *Harry Feldman* made his major league debut in this Pittsburgh stadium...?

419. ► This Jewish third baseman had 123 RBI for the 1893 pennant-winning Boston Beaneaters...?

420. ► Name 2 of the 3 Jewish players who participated in the 1939 Hall of Fame Dedication Game at Cooperstown, New York...?

JEWISH BASEBALL NEWS   Special

HERTZ SIGNS FOR $50,000

Third baseman *Steve Hertz* was one of the first 'bonus babies,' signing on the dotted line in 1963 for the expansion Houston Colt .45s.

"You had a better opportunity then because if you shined at that time you could bargain," the one-time Miami High School standout said recently.

"There were a lot of clubs, and you could play one against the other."

This was several seasons before the draft which assigned high school or college graduates to a team before any bargaining could be done.

"Houston was an expansion team, and they were willing to come up with a little more money than the other clubs," he added.

In his case, the little 'bonus' was fifty big ones ($50,000).

Despite his rich-baseball rookie status, Steve didn't see much action in the major leagues as a player.

Born February 26, 1945, in Dayton, Ohio, the eldest son of David and Sara Hertz, natives of St. Louis, Missouri, he moved with his family to Miami, Florida, early in life. He suited up for the Colts in '64, fanned in his first at bat against John Tsitouris, then was shipped off to Durham, North

Due to team name change, *Steve Hertz* signs for Houston Colt .45s and suits up for Astros.

Carolina in the Carolina League.

His 'bonus' status, however, was not so far off the mark. Wherever he went he was always an excellent third baseman with a healthy bat. Following Durham, Steve played for Cocoa in the Florida State League where he made the All-Star Team as a third baseman.

He was on the year-end All-Star team the following year. This time for Salisbury, North Carolina in the Western Carolinas League.

After he left the Astros' system ('67), he tied a Midwest League record for assists by a third

Dan Stearns poses with Cincinnati teammates (back row, left to right) Harry McCormick, Phil Powers, *Dan,* Bid McPhee; (middle row) Hick Carpenter, Pop Snyder, Will White, Chick Fulmer, Joe Sommer; (bottom row) Jimmy Macullar and Harry Wheeler for 1882 American Association champion's team photo.

baseman in one game, as a member of the Dodgers' farm club in Dubuque, Iowa.

His last years as a player were with High Point, North Carolina, in the Carolina League; as a player/coach for Pompano Beach in the Florida State League; and with Tidewater, Virginia, in the International League.

But Steve had a 'kicker' in his bonus contract. During the off season he could attend college. His choice was the University of Miami, from which he graduated with a B.A. in Education in 1969. He later obtained a Master's degree from Nova University.

When he took off his player's uniform and picked up his second sheepskin, Steve suited up in a coach's pinstripes. Since 1970, he has been a teacher and baseball coach in the Miami area, winning over 300 games, including a state championship (Coral Park High, 1978) and state runner-up (Southridge High, 1984).

He resides with his wife, Fran Sokol, and their two children, Jeffrey and Darren.

When asked if he would become a bonus baby again, Steve laughed and said, "I would probably do it the same way."

That same way would probably mean the fifty big ones would have at least another zero at the end. And for an excellent third baseman that figure of $500,000 would have looked awfully good.

189

ANSWERS

415. ► Pud Galvin. On August 20, 1880, in a National League game at Buffalo, *Stearns* played third base for the winning Buffalo Bisons. Dude Esterbrook's first-inning triple scored Joe Hornung with the only run of the game. The Bisons defeated the Worcester Nationals, 1-0. Losing pitcher Fred Corey allowed 4 hits.

416. ► Mel Harder. On September 20, 1934, Harder's 7-hitter bested *Cohen*, as the Cleveland Indians defeated the Washington Senators, at League Park, 6-1. Earl Averill homered for the Indians.

417. ► Mike Caldwell. On September 19, 1975, the San Diego Padres right fielder singled in 4 at bats. Caldwell yielded 5 hits, as the San Francisco Giants defeated the Padres, at Candlestick Park, 3-1. Randy Jones was the losing pitcher. *Sharon* had 102 hits and a .218 career batting average.

418. ► Forbes Field. On September 10, 1941, the New York Giants rookie allowed 5 hits and was relieved in the seventh inning when the Pirates scored 5 runs. Johnny Lanning was the winning pitcher, as the Pittsburgh Pirates defeated the Giants, 10-7. Bill Lohrman took the loss.

419. ► *Billy Nash.*

420. ► *Morrie Arnovich, Moe Berg* and *Hank Greenberg.*

HALL
OF
FAME

421. ► This Jewish hurler was the last Brooklyn Dodgers pitcher to appear in a game prior to the team's transfer to Los Angeles...?

ALL-STARS

422. ► This Indians pitcher assisted in stopping Joe DiMaggio's hitting streak at 56 games and a year later surrendered *Murray Franklin*'s first major league home run...?

1960-
PRESENT

423. ► Although this Reds Jewish outfielder had only 54 hits in 1966, he homered 21 times...?

1930-59

424. ► *Cal Abrams* had 6 hits and a .143 batting average in 17 games with the 1954 Pittsburgh Pirates, including 4 hits in 1 game in this Chicago stadium...?

OLD-TIMERS
1857-1929

425. ► This Jewish first baseman was the first-ever Milwaukee player to hit a home run...?

BASEBALL
MISCELLANY

426. ► He was the Jewish author of *The Great All-Time Baseball Record Book*...?

(Answers next page.)

ANSWERS

421. ► *Sandy Koufax.* On September 29, 1957, reliever *Koufax* hurled a scoreless eighth inning. Seth Morehead yielded 4 hits, as the Philadelphia Phillies defeated the Brooklyn Dodgers, at Connie Mack Stadium, 2-1. Roger Craig was the losing pitcher.

ALL-STARS

422. ► Al Smith. On May 29, 1942, in the fourth inning, the Detroit Tigers shortstop, *Murray Franklin*, hit a 2-run homer. Hal White gave up 13 hits, as the Tigers defeated the Cleveland Indians, at Briggs Stadium, 14-3. *Franklin* had 43 hits, including 2 home runs, and a .262 career batting average.

1960-
PRESENT

423. ► *Art Shamsky.*

1930-59

424. ► Wrigley Field. On May 2, 1954, in the second game of a doubleheader, the Pittsburgh Pirates left fielder had 4 hits, including a double and triple, scored 4 runs and had 1 RBI. Bob Friend, with relief help from John Hetki, was the winning pitcher, as the Pirates defeated the Chicago Cubs, 18-10. Bubba Church took the loss.

OLD-TIMERS
1857-1929

425. ► *Jake Goodman.* On June 25, 1878, in the third inning, the Milwaukee Cream Citys first baseman had his only major league home run. Harry Wheeler yielded 7 hits, as the Providence Grays defeated the Cream Citys, 11-4. Mike Golden was the losing pitcher. Providence made 18 of the game's 35 errors, including 9 by pitcher Wheeler.

BASEBALL
MISCELLANY

426. ► *Joseph L. Reichler.*

HALL
OF
FAME

427. ► This Jewish Hall of Famer had 7 100-RBI seasons...?

ALL-STARS

428. ► In 1949, George Munger hurled a 1-hitter, allowing only a single to this Giants Jewish third baseman...?

1960-
PRESENT

429. ► *Jeff Newman* caught 1 victory in the 1981 American League West Division Play-offs hurled by this ERA leader...?

1930-59

430. ► This manager of the 1961 pennant-winning Cincinnati Reds surrendered *Duke Markell*'s only major league hit...?

OLD-TIMERS
1857-1929

431. ► In 1915, outfielder *Sam Mayer* made his only appearance as a pitcher in this Washington stadium...?

BASEBALL
MISCELLANY

432. ► Nick Altrock, *Max Patkin* and the San Diego Chicken have what in common?

(Answers next page.)

ANSWERS

HALL
OF
FAME

427. ► *Hank Greenberg.* His 100-plus RBI seasons were 1934-35, 1937-40, and 1946.

ALL-STARS

428. ► *Sid Gordon.* On September 13, 1949, in the second inning, Gordon singled. Munger won his fourteenth game, as the St. Louis Cardinals defeated the New York Giants, at Sportsman's Park, 1-0. Dave Koslo was the losing pitcher.

1960-
PRESENT

429. ► Steve McCatty. On October 7, 1981, McCatty yielded 6 hits, as his Oakland Athletics defeated the Kansas City Royals, at Royals Stadium, 2-1. Mike Jones took the loss. Tony Armas had 4 hits and 2 runs batted in.

1930-59

430. ► Fred Hutchinson. On September 27, 1951, the St. Louis Browns pitcher doubled and scored. Markell was the winning pitcher, as the Browns defeated the Detroit Tigers, at Sportsman's Park, 7-4.

OLD-TIMERS
1857-1929

431. ► American League Park. On September 17, 1915, the Washington Senators used pitchers Joe Boehling, Doc Ayers, *Sam Mayer* and George Dumont. *Mayer* entered the game in the seventh inning, allowed 2 walks and was then relieved by Dumont. Tim McCabe yielded 5 hits, as the St. Louis Browns defeated the Senators, 9-0. John Henry was the Senators catcher.

BASEBALL
MISCELLANY

432. ► They are baseball entertainers.

433. ▶ *Sandy Koufax* fanned this Hall of Fame 300-game winner for his first World Series strikeout . . . ?

434. ▶ In 1950, this Jewish rookie had 116 RBI . . . ?

435. ▶ In 1972, *Mike Epstein* appeared in his first World Series game against this Reds hurler, who led the National League in pitching percentage and had a 1.99 ERA . . . ?

436. ▶ Sid Gautreaux caught this Dodgers Jewish pitcher's first major league victory in 1936 . . . ?

437. ▶ Hall of Famer Eddie Collins had 743 career stolen bases and 14 thefts in the World Series. He was thrown out by this Cubs Jewish catcher while attempting to steal a base for the first time in a World Series game . . . ?

438. ▶ In 1955, the Cincinnati Reds signed this Jewish outfielder to a bonus contract . . . ?

(Answers next page.)

ANSWERS

433. ► Early Wynn. On October 1, 1959, in the fifth inning of the first game, Wynn was called out on strikes. Reliever *Koufax* retired 6 consecutive batters in 2 innings. Wynn was the winning pitcher, as the Chicago White Sox defeated the Los Angeles Dodgers, at Comiskey Park, 11-0. Roger Craig took the loss. Ted Kluszewski hit 2 home runs.

434. ► *Al Rosen.*

435. ► Gary Nolan. On October 14, 1972, in the first game, the Oakland Athletics first baseman had no hits in 3 at bats and a walk. *Ken Holtzman* was the winning pitcher, as the Athletics defeated the Cincinnati Reds, at Riverfront Stadium, 3-2. A's catcher Gene Tenace hit 2 home runs.

436. ► *Harry Eisenstat.* On September 24, 1936, in the second game of a doubleheader at Ebbets Field, the Brooklyn Dodgers rookie singled in 2 at-bats and won his first game. *Eisenstat* yielded 7 hits, as the Dodgers defeated the Philadelphia Phillies, in a game called after 6½ innings, 4-2. Reliever Hal Kelleher was the losing pitcher.

437. ► *Johnny Kling.* On October 17, 1910, in the first inning of the first game, the Philadelphia Athletics second baseman singled and was then caught stealing, *Kling* to Joe Tinker. Chief Bender yielded 3 hits, as the Athletics defeated the Chicago Cubs, at Shibe Park, 4-1. Orvie Overall took the loss. In 1910, Collins had a league-leading 81-stolen bases.

438. ► *Al Silvera.*

HALL
OF
FAME

439. ► *Hank Greenberg* had his last career hit in this Pittsburgh stadium...?

ALL-STARS

440. ► In 1969, *Art Shamsky* made his first World Series appearance and batted against this Orioles Cy Young Award winner...?

1960-
PRESENT

441. ► In 1973, this Astros Jewish player had 10 hits and a .323 batting average as a pinch-hitter...?

1930-59

442. ► This hurler, nicknamed "the Count of Luxemburg," surrendered *Phil Weintraub*'s first major league hit...?

OLD-TIMERS
1857-1929

443. ► In 1897, Willie Sudhoff surrendered this Bridegrooms Jewish first baseman's only major league home run...?

BASEBALL
MISCELLANY

444. ► Authors *Bernard Postal, Jessie Silver* and *Roy Silver* wrote a sports book called...?

CHOZEN BLASTS 46-GAME RECORD

Harry Chozen stood in the on-deck circle, waiting patiently for Mobile teammate Pete Thomassie to swing.

Behind him was a 32-game batting streak. Ahead was the Southern Association league's 46-consecutive game record of Nashville's Johnny Bates that had withstood countless challenges over 20 years.

The Memphis pitcher hurled the ball... A whiff...

"I couldn't let the tension get to me," Harry recalls. "I had to concentrate on what I was going to do."

What he had already done in the minors was an indication of a mighty bat.

Harry is the sixth of 7 children born to Abraham and Ida Chozen, His parents were born and raised in Podolia Gubernie, in the Ukraine, where his older brother and sister were born. His father brought the family to the United States in 1903-04, and settled in Winnebago, Minnesota, where Harry was born September 27, 1915. It wasn't easy for his father who worked in the junk, metal, and fur businesses. "We were the only Jewish family in a Swedish town," Harry recalls.

In 1923, the family moved to Southern California where Harry attended Washington Junior High School and Pasadena Junior College.

In 1933, he left school to pursue a baseball career as a catcher, went to San Antonio, Texas, but failed to make the team.

Two years after studying under Dizzy and Daffy Dean at a baseball school in Hot Springs, Arkansas, he batted .321 for Lake Charles, Louisiana, in the Evangeline League (1935).

He had a .342 batting average in his second season with El Dorado, Arkansas, in the Cotton States League. On the strength of that average he was voted the Most Valuable Player.

This had garnered for him a shot at the majors with the Cincinnati Reds.

Standing there in the on-deck circle, he watched as the pitcher wound up... Another whiff...

In his appearance he had caught Joe Cascarella and Bill Hallahan, and singled off Phillies pitcher Wayne LaMaster.

"I hit a line drive between short and third."

With the Reds he wore the uniform of recently-released manager Charlie Dressen.

"Whenever I went on the field, I was booed," he recalls from Lake Charles, Louisiana, where he lives with his second wife Ruth Stern-

...erg and sells real estate and insurance.

His one shot over, he turned his baseball attention to minor league records.

"I was too far away from the record to think about it during that game. Just getting a hit was important. I was a contact hitter and struck out rarely."

All he wanted were his chances at-bat.

He had plenty of chances in the years between his 1-game stint with the Reds, September 21, 1937, and that day in 1945 when the record was 14 games away.

This time waiting his turn at bat, Harry watched the fastball again whiff the batter. But that bat slipped out of Thomassie's hand and came flying toward him.

Although he lunged away from the flight of the bat, he was struck on the head, knocked unconscious and had to be taken out of the game.

The streak was over...

For 3 years he played for Albany, New York, in the Eastern League, and had 1 year wearing the uniform of Williamsport, Pennsylvania, also in the Eastern, League before becoming player-manager of Newport News in the Virginia League.

(His brother Bobby played briefly with Newport News. Another brother, Myer, also played in the minor leagues from '32-42.)

Then it was on to Knoxville, Tennessee, which had transferred him to Mobile—and his chance at the record.

Harry Chozen hit safely in 49 consecutive minor league games.

By leaving the game, the streak was over at 32 games. Or so it appeared, until Southern Association President Billy Evans ruled that due to the accident occurring before Harry had an official at-bat (he had walked earlier in the game) the streak was still intact.

The next game Harry hit safely. He was to continue hitting safely for the next 16 games, to set the record of 49 games, this despite being used 4 times as a pinch-hitter or late-inning replacement when he had only 1 at-bat in each game.

For the next 6 years he turned his talents to managing, and was a player-manager with Greenville, Mississippi, and Pine Bluff, Arkansas, in the Cotton States League, Miami Beach in the Florida International League, and with Lake Charles in the Evangeline League.

Harry can't forget that streak.

"I was proud of my years in baseball and proud of my Jewish heritage," he added.

ANSWERS

439. ▶ Forbes Field. On September 15, 1947, in the sixth inning, the Pittsburgh Pirates first baseman hit a solo home run off Charley Schanz. Kirby Higbe yielded 8 hits, as the Pirates defeated the Philadelphia Phillies, 12-2. Tommy Hughes was the losing pitcher. *Greenberg* had 331 home runs, 1628 hits and a .313 career batting average.

440. ▶ Mike Cuellar. On October 11, 1969, in the ninth inning of the first game, *Shamsky* pinch-hit for pitcher Ron Taylor and grounded out to end the game. Cuellar yielded 6 hits, as the Baltimore Orioles defeated the New York Mets, at Memorial Stadium, 4-1. Tom Seaver took the loss.

441. ▶ *Norm Miller.*

442. ▶ Heine Meine. On September 7, 1933, the New York Giants rookie, *Weintraub,* replaced Lefty O'Doul in right field. In the sixth inning he belted a solo homer. Meine surrendered 10 hits as the Pittsburgh Pirates defeated the Giants, at Forbes Field, 14-2. Roy Parmelee was the losing pitcher.

443. ▶ *Broadway Smith.* On August 20, 1897, the Brooklyn Bridegrooms first baseman had the only home run of his career, 1897-1906. Jack Dunn yielded 11 hits, as the Bridegrooms defeated the St. Louis Browns, at Eastern Park, 12-7. Red Donahue took the loss.

444. ▶ *Encyclopedia of Jews in Sports.*

Baseball Judaica

QUESTIONS

HALL
OF
FAME

445. ▶ In a 1965 game, Jim Hickman's homer was the only hit allowed by this Dodgers Jewish hurler...?

ALL-STARS

446. ▶ In 1950, this hurler, nicknamed "Sugar," surrendered *Al Rosen's* league-leading thirty-seventh home run...?

1960-
PRESENT

447. ▶ This Jewish outfielder played for 6 different teams in his 8 seasons between 1965-1974...?

1930-59

448. ▶ Pitcher *Harry Feldman* had his first career home run in this Chicago stadium...?

OLD-TIMERS
1857-1929

449. ▶ In 1929, Johnny Prudhomme surrendered a grand slam home run to this Senators Jewish second baseman...?

BASEBALL
MISCELLANY

450. ▶ Outfielder *Morrie Arnovich* was a member of the 1940 World Champion Cincinnati Reds—which was managed by this Hall of Famer...?

(Answers next page.)

ANSWERS

445. ▶ *Sandy Koufax.* On June 20, 1965, in the fifth inning of the first game of a doubleheader, Hickman belted a homer. *Koufax* went on to strike out 12 batters and allowed 2 walks, as the Los Angeles Dodgers defeated the New York Mets, at Dodger Stadium, 2-1. Warren Spahn was the losing pitcher.

446. ▶ Bob Cain. On September 26, 1950, in the second inning, the Cleveland Indians third baseman, *Rosen,* lofted one into the stands. Early Wynn yielded 6 hits in winning his 18th game of the season. The Indians defeated the Chicago White Sox, at Municipal Stadium, 2-0.

447. ▶ *Richie Scheinblum.* He played for Cleveland, Washington, Kansas City, Cincinnati, California, and St. Louis.

448. ▶ Wrigley Field. On May 1, 1942, in the fourth inning, the New York Giants reliever hit a solo homer off Jake Mooty. Tot Pressnell was the winning pitcher, as the Chicago Cubs defeated the Giants, 13-9. Losing pitcher Hugh East also homered.

449. ▶ *Buddy Myer.* On August 5, 1929, in the sixth inning, the Washington Senators second baseman had an inside-the-park grand slam home run. *Myer* had 4 hits, 7 runs batted in, 1 stolen base and scored 4 runs in this memorable game. Lloyd Brown yielded 10 hits, as the Senators defeated the Detroit Tikgers, at Griffith Stadium, 21-5. George Uhle took the loss.

450. ▶ Bill McKechnie.

451. ► Pitcher *Bo Belinsky* surrendered this Braves Hall of Famer's 400th career home run . . . ?

452. ► This Cardinals hurler, a 21-game winner in 1960, surrendered *Larry Sherry's* first major league home run . . . ?

453. ► This Cubs Jewish hurler holds the National League record for most wins in an undefeated season . . . ?

454. ► In 1931, *Alta Cohen* debuted in this Boston stadium . . . ?

455. ► In a 1909 game, Mike Mowrey's single was the only hit allowed by which Cubs Jewish hurler . . . ?

456. ► These Jewish brothers were catchers in the major leagues. The oldest brother appeared in 2 games with the 1928 St. Louis Browns and the youngest had a 10-year career with the New York Giants . . . ?

(Answers next page.)

ANSWERS

451. ► Hank Aaron. On April 20, 1966, in the ninth inning, the Atlanta Braves right fielder and baseball's career home run king belted a solo home run. Aaron also blasted a homer in the first inning off losing pitcher Ray Culp. Ken Johnson yielded 6 hits, as the Braves defeated the Philadelphia Phillies, at Connie Mack Stadium, 8-1.

452. ► Ernie Broglio. On August 15, 1959, the Los Angeles Dodgers hurler had 3 hits, including an RBI single in the second inning and a 2-run homer in the fifth. *Sherry* relieved Johnny Podres and hurled 8⅔ scoreless innings, as the Dodgers defeat of the St. Louis Cardinals, at Busch Stadium, 4-3. Duke Snider's sixth inning homer won the game.

453. ► *Ken Holtzman* was 9-0 in 1967.

454. ► Braves Field. On April 15, 1931, in the fifth inning. Ike Boone batted for the Brooklyn Robins pitcher and then replaced Babe Herman in right field. Boone returned to the dugout and *Cohen* went to right field. In the sixth inning, *Cohen* batted out of turn in Herman's third position and singled. The error was discovered too late to void the hit. In the next inning, *Cohen* batted in the ninth position, singled and later scored. Harry Seibold yielded 8 hits, as the Boston Braves defeated the Robins, 9-3. Sloppy Thurston took the loss. *Cohen* threw out 2 base-runners.

455. ► *Ed Reulbach.* On June 26, 1909, *Reulbach* had 3 strikeouts and issued 1 walk, as the Chicago Cubs defeated the Cincinnati Reds, at West Side Park, 4-0. Bill Campbell was the losing pitcher.

456. ► *Ike* and *Harry Danning.*

457. ▶ This Hall of Famer holds the National League record for the most home runs in his final season . . . ?

458. ▶ Ralph Branca is best remembered as the pitcher who surrendered a home run to Bobby Thomson to end the 1951 season. In his 1944 debut, Branca yielded a homer to this Giants Jewish first baseman . . . ?

459. ▶ In a 1975 game, Johnny Grubb's bunt single was the only hit allowed by the combined hurling of this Cubs Jewish pitcher and Tom Dettore . . . ?

460. ▶ This hurler won a 16-0 game in his debut and 2 years later surrendered *Chick Starr's* first major league hit . . . ?

461. ▶ In 1870, this hurler stopped the Cincinnati Red Stockings 130-game winning streak, and the following year was the opposing pitcher in *Nate Berkenstock's* only game in the National Association of Professional Baseball Players . . . ?

462. ▶ He is the Jewish author of *A Season in the Sun*—a book dealing with baseball . . . ?

ANSWERS

HALL
OF
FAME

457. ► *Hank Greenberg* had 25 home runs in 1947.

ALL-STARS

458. ► *Phil Weintraub.* On June 12, 1944, the New York Giants first baseman had a 3-run homer off Wes Flowers and a solo homer off Branca. *Weintraub* also singled, had 3 walks, 5 RBI and scored 5 runs. Bill Voiselle was the winning pitcher, as the Giants defeated the Brooklyn Dodgers, at the Polo Grounds, 15-9. Cal McLish took the loss.

1960-
PRESENT

459. ► *Steve Stone.* On July 19, 1975, in the sixth inning, *Stone* issued bases-loaded walks to Dave Winfield and Mike Ivie. Following Grubb's seventh inning 2-out bunt single, Dettore relieved and allowed no hits. Dave Freisleben yielded 6 hits, as the San Diego Padres defeated the Chicago Cubs, at San Diego Stadium, 2-1. *Stone* had 5 strikeouts and issued 9 walks.

1930-59

460. ► Russ Van Atta. On August 27, 1935, in the fifth inning of the second game of a doubleheader, the Washington Senators catcher singled and later scored. Van Atta yielded 9 hits, as the St. Louis Browns defeated the Senators, at Sportsman's Park, 11-1. Bobo Newsom was the losing pitcher.

OLD-TIMERS
1857-1929

461. ► George Zettlein. On October 30, 1871, on the final day of the season, the Philadelphia Athletics right fielder had no hits in 4 at-bats. Dick McBride yielded 4 hits, as the Athletics defeated the Chicago White Stockings, at Brooklyn's Union Grounds, 4-1.

BASEBALL
MISCELLANY

462. ► *Roger Kahn.*

HALL
OF
FAME

463. ► In 1965, this Jewish hurler made 20 of his 75 career hits . . . ?

ALL-STARS

464. ► In 1973, this Cubs third baseman singled for the only hit allowed by *Ken Holtzman* in an All-Star Game . . . ?

1960-
PRESENT

465. ► Who was the Pirates All-Star reliever that surrendered *Norm Miller*'s only career grand slam home run . . . ?

1930-59

466. ► In 1949, Tigers catcher *Joe Ginsberg* debuted in this stadium . . . ?

OLD-TIMERS
1857-1929

467. ► In a 1914 game, Dots Miller singled for the only hit allowed by this Phillies Jewish 21-game winner . . . ?

BASEBALL
MISCELLANY

468. ► In 1963, umpire *Al Forman* was assigned to home plate when this New York Mets hurler finally won a game after 18 consecutive defeats . . . ?

(Answers on page 210.)

COHEN ENDS MUSIAL'S SLUMP

After 7 years in the minors, *Hy Cohen* finally had his chance at the major leagues when called to relief duty for the Chicago Cubs against the St. Louis Cardinals.

That was in the Spring of 1955 and followed a 16-6 season with Des Moines, Iowa, in the Western League. He had led the league with a 1.88 ERA and had 2 play-off victories.

For his efforts, the league had voted him their Most Valuable Player and selected him to the All-Star team.

Walking to the mound in relief, his early career flashed through his mind.

Born January 29, 1931, to Joseph, who came from Warsaw, Poland, and Bessie, from Brest Litovsk, Russia, Hy was a pitcher in Brooklyn's Prospect Park leagues before signing to play professional baseball.

Working under a New York Yankees minor league contract, he had hurled for LaGrange in the Georgia-Alabama League where he was 7-5 in '48, and 11-15 the next season.

The Chicago Cubs drafted Hy and placed him in their minor league farm system.

His work on the mound that season, '50, had given him a 12-9 record with Grand Rapids, Michigan, in the Central League.

Still with dreams of the majors,

Hy had been assigned to De Moines, Iowa, the next season. 16-10 record with a 2.86 ERA an 3 play-off victories raised the ey brows of more than one majo league manager.

They had to wait 2 years befor they could look at him again. Th was while he served out his assign ment in the military. However, h still found time to suit up with th likes of Bobby Brown, Bob Turley Marv Rotblatt, Don Newcombe Dick Kokos, Gus Triandos, Jc Margoneri and Owen Friend a base camp in San Antonio, Texa

He reported to the Los Angele Angels (not the expansion team but a member of the Pacific Coas League). After pitching a few in nings, the Cubs shipped him off t Des Moines, again.

Prove himself there, and he ha a shot at the big time.

Prove himself he did, with h 1.88 ERA.

By the time he stood on th mound in that relief game, he wa as ready as he would ever be.

"Stan Musial thanked me fo getting him out of his slump," H recalls somewhat humorousl from his home in the San Fe nando Valley.

In that first game, the Cardina belted him for 12 hits and 8 runs 7 innings.

He still appeared in another games, but had no decisions, ar

Despite being belted for 12 hits and 8 runs in 7 innings in his first major league game, *Hy Cohen* laughingly recalls that he ended Stan Musial's slump.

ERA of 7.94.

His one shot in the majors had proven a disaster, but Hy still had hat it takes.

He finished the season with the ngels (5-10) and in 1956 was 6-0 ith the Angels before being sold New Orleans in the Southern ssociation, where he won 15 and st 7.

His ability to keep the runs own continued through a year ith Memphis, also in the South-n Association ('57), where he led e league in ERA.

But the magic that kept his ball oating was gone by the next year —during which he earned his largest paycheck—while hurling for Toronto in the International League.

He retired to attend Brooklyn College, before transferring to California State in Los Angeles. He was graduated with a Bachelor's degree in Education in '61, and received a Master's from California State in Northridge in '66.

Hy is married to Terry Davis, and they have two children. In addition to teaching history, the former physical education teacher also coaches the football, tennis *and* baseball teams.

ANSWERS

463. ► *Sandy Koufax.*

464. ► Ron Santo. On July 24, 1973, in the second inning, the Oakland Athletics pitcher replaced Catfish Hunter, who was injured. *Holtzman* allowed a single in two-thirds of an inning. Rick Wise was the winning pitcher, as the National League defeated the American League, at Royals Stadium, Kansas City, 7-1. Bert Blyleven took the loss.

465. ► Roy Face. On August 10, 1968, in the eighth inning of the first game of a doubleheader, *Miller*, the Houston Astros right fielder, hit a grand slam homer. Reliever Danny Coombs was the winning pitcher, as the Astros defeated the Pittsburgh Pirates, at the Astrodome, 16-3. Steve Blass took the loss.

466. ► Briggs Stadium, Detroit. On September 15, 1948, the Detroit Tigers catcher had 1 hit in 4 plate appearances and scored the winning run. Lou Kretlow yielded 9 hits, as the Tigers defeated the Washington Senators, 4-2. Milo Candini was the losing pitcher.

467. ► *Erskine Mayer.* On July 27, 1914, in the second game of a doubleheader, *Mayer* allowed only a single to the St. Louis Cardinals shortstop. The Philadelphia Phillies defeated the Cardinals, at Baker Bowl, 2-0. Dan Griner took the loss. *Mayer* doubled and scored 1 run.

468. ► Roger Craig.

HALL
OF
FAME

469. ► *Ed Reulbach* was the first pitcher to strike out this Hall of Famer nicknamed "Wahoo Sam" in a World Series game...?

ALL-STARS

470. ► This Yankees outfielder and manager of the 1966 World Series Champion Baltimore Orioles was retired by second baseman *Al Federoff* for the final out in Virgil Trucks second no-hitter in 1952...?

1960-
PRESENT

471. ► In 1969, *Lloyd Allen* debuted in this Washington stadium...?

1930-59

472. ► Name 3 of the 4 Jewish players on the 1941 New York Giants?

OLD-TIMERS
1857-1929

473. ► In 1884, Dave Foutz yielded this Jewish third baseman's first major league home run...?

BASEBALL
MISCELLANY

474. ► This Chicago Cubs stockholder originated the plan that led to the creation of the Office of the Baseball Commissioner...?

(Answers next page.)

ANSWERS

469. ► Sam Crawford. On October 8, 1907, in the tenth inning of the first game at West Side Park, *Reulbach,* the Chicago Cubs hurler, relieved Orvie Overall and fanned the Detroit Tigers center fielder. *Reulbach* blanked the Tigers in 3 innings. After twelve innings, the game was called because of darkness with the score tied at 3-3. Tigers pitcher Wild Bill Donovan yielded 10 hits.

ALL-STARS

470. ► Hank Bauer. On August 25, 1952, Bauer grounded to the Detroit Tigers second baseman, who threw to Walt Dropo at first for the final out. The Tigers defeated the New York Yankees, at Yankee Stadium, 1-0. Bill Miller took the loss.

1960-
PRESENT

471. ► Robert F. Kennedy Stadium. On September 1, 1969, in the first game of a doubleheader, the California Angels reliever hurled a scoreless seventh inning. Joe Coleman yielded 9 hits, as the Washington Senators defeated the Angels, 4-0. *Mike Epstein* had 4 hits, including a 3-run homer. Tom Murphy was the losing pitcher.

1930-59

472. ► *Morrie Arnovich, Harry Danning, Harry Feldman* and *Sid Gordon.*

OLD-TIMERS
1857-1929

473. ► *Billy Nash.* On September 15, 1884, in the first inning, the Richmond Virginias third baseman hit the first of his 61 career home runs. Bob Caruthers was the winning pitcher, as the St. Louis Browns defeated the Virginias, in an American Association game at Sportsman's Park, 7-6. Ed Dugan took the loss. Foutz had 147 career victories, 66 defeats and a .690 pitching percentage.

BASEBALL
MISCELLANY

474. ► *Albert Lasker.*

475. ► *Norm Sherry* debuted and caught this Jewish Hall of Famer...?

476. ► In 1953, this Jewish catcher scored on *Al Rosen's* 145th league-leading RBI of the season...?

477. ► This Jewish outfielder/first baseman had 6 career pinch-hit home runs between 1965 and 1972...?

478. ► Pitcher *Bud Swartz* made his major league debut in this St. Louis stadium...?

479. ► In 1914, George Davis surrendered this Phillies Jewish hurler's first major league home run...?

480. ► Who was the Jewish author of *Clowning Through Baseball*?

(Answers next page.)

ANSWERS

475. ► *Sandy Koufax.* On April 12, 1959, *Koufax,* Johnny Klippstein (who got credit for the win), and Clem Labine each hurled three innings. Don Demeter's seventh inning, 2-run homer won the game. The Los Angeles Dodgers defeated the Chicago Cubs, at Wrigley Field, 5-3. *Sherry* had a 2-run single off losing pitcher Taylor Phillips.

476. ► *Joe Ginsberg.* On September 27, 1953, in the third inning of the season finale, the Cleveland Indians catcher doubled and scored on *Rosen's* hit. *Rosen* had 3 hits, including a double, and scored 2 runs. Al Aber yielded 9 hits, as the Detroit Tigers defeated the Indians, at Municipal Stadium, 7-3. Bob Feller took the loss. That year, *Rosen's* 43 home runs, 115 runs and .613 slugging percentage were also league-leading totals.

477. ► *Art Shamsky.*

478. ► Sportsman's Park. On July 12, 1947, in the first game of a doubleheader, the St. Louis Browns reliever hurled a scoreless ninth inning. Butch Wensloff was the winning pitcher, as the New York Yankees defeated the Browns, 12-2. Bob Muncrief took the loss. This was the Yankees' eleventh consecutive victory. Joe DiMaggio and Billy Johnson homered.

479. ► *Erskine Mayer.* On July 1, 1914, in the first game of a doubleheader, the Philadelphia Phillies pitcher homered. *Mayer* yielded 6 hits, as the Phillies defeated the Boston Braves, at South End Grounds, 7-2.

480. ► *Al Schacht.*

HALL
OF
FAME
481. ► In the 1934 World Series, this two-time National League ERA leader surrendered two doubles to *Hank Greenberg*...?

ALL-STARS
482. ► In 1939, this Phillies Jewish outfielder had his best season, batting .324...?

1960-
PRESENT
483. ► In 1962, Norm Bass surrendered this Angels hurler's first major league hit...?

1930-59
484. ► Shortstop *Eddie Feinberg* tied a fielding record when he had no chances in a 12-inning game in this Cincinnati stadium...?

OLD-TIMERS
1857-1929
485. ► In 1908, Jack Hannifan scored the last run off this Cubs Jewish pitcher who ended the season with 44 consecutive scoreless innings...?

BASEBALL
MISCELLANY
486. ► What does *Steve Stone* have in common with Joe Nuxhall and Phil Rizzuto?

(Answers next page.)

ANSWERS

HALL
OF
FAME

481. ► Bill Walker. On October 6, 1934, in the fourth game, the Detroit Tigers first baseman had 4 hits, including run-scoring doubles in the seventh and eighth innings. Eldon Auker yielded 10 hits, as the Tigers defeated the St. Louis Cardinals, at Sportsman's Park, 10-4. *Greenberg* led the league with 63 doubles.

ALL-STARS

482. ► *Morrie Arnovich.*

1960-
PRESENT

483. ► *Bo Belinsky.* On April 18, 1962, the Los Angeles Angels pitcher debuted and his fourth inning single scored Eddie Yost with the winning run. Belinsky, with relief help from Art Fowler, was also the winning pitcher. The Angels defeated the Kansas City Athletics, at Chavez Ravine, 3-2.

1930-59

484. ► Crosley Field. On May 19, 1939, *Feinberg,* the Philadelphia Phillies shortstop, had 2 hits and did not have a chance in the field. Ernie Lombardi's twelfth-inning homer ended the game. Paul Derringer yielded 10 hits, as the Cincinnati Reds defeated the Phillies, 4-3. Max Butcher took the loss.

OLD-TIMERS
1857-1929

485. ► *Ed Reulbach.* On September 17, 1908, in the seventh inning, the Boston Doves shortstop scored a run. *Reulbach* yielded 12 hits, as the Chicago Cubs defeated the Doves, at South End Grounds, 4-1. Tom Tuckey was the losing pitcher. *Reulbach* had 2 hits, including a double.

BASEBALL
MISCELLANY

486. ► They are former big leaguers who became base-ball announcers.

HALL
OF
FAME
487. ▶ In 1919, this White Sox Hall of Famer caught *Erskine Mayer*'s 91st and last major league victory . . . ?

ALL-STARS
488. ▶ Dodgers pitcher *Larry Sherry* won his first major league game in this stadium . . . ?

1960-
PRESENT
489. ▶ This former Tigers batting champion made the last out in 2 of *Sandy Koufax'* no-hitters . . . ?

1930-59
490. ▶ This Tigers 3-time, 20-game winner (1934-1936) surrendered *Jim Levey*'s first major league home run . . . ?

OLD-TIMERS
1857-1929
491. ▶ In a 1916 game, this Giants Jewish outfielder's inside-the-park grand slam home run backed Ferdie Schupp's 1-hitter . . . ?

BASEBALL
MISCELLANY
492. ▶ Who is the Jewish author of *Great Jews in Sports*?

(Answers on page 220.)

IT COULD HAVE BEEN GREAT

"But for the Grace of God, it could have been great," says *Cal Abrams.*

He was the rookie Brooklyn Dodgers outfielder who was tagged out at the plate in the 1950 season finale, which the Philadelphia Phillies won.

"Robin Roberts had walked me, and I was on second base. Tie score," he recalls. "Stan Lopata gave a sign to pick me off. Roberts missed the sign and pitched the ball. Duke Snider hit a line drive right by me. I was waived around third."

Had he made it he would have been the winning run.

"Richie Ashburn, who had been charging in to back up the play, caught the ball on one bounce behind second base and got rid of it fast.

"The ball was already in the catcher's glove. I ran into Stan Lopata who was standing way up on the baseline. He almost killed me."

The Phillies won the game and the pennant on a 3-run homer by Dick Sisler in the tenth inning.

Cal, the oldest of three children of Marcus and Ethel, was born March 2, 1924, in Philadelphia, Pennsylvania. His father, a native of Omsk, Russia, was in the trucking business while his mother came from Atlantic City, New Jersey.

Brooklyn Dodgers lefty *Cal Abrams* practice swing.

The family moved to Brooklyn where Cal attended New Utrecht, Lafayette, Abraham Lincoln and James Madison High Schools. He played first base and outfield for James Madison before graduating in 1941.

He was signed to a professional baseball contract by Brooklyn Dodgers scout Joe Labate. Cal reported to Olean, New York, in the Pony League, and two weeks later was drafted into the U.S. Army, serving in Greenland and the Philippines.

In '46, following his military discharge, he was then assigned to Danville, Illinois, in the Three-I League.

For the next 2 seasons, Cal played for Mobile (the '47 pennant winners) in the Southern Association.

"I was a very good minor league player. I hit in the .330s and .340s," he recalls.

He began the '49 season with the Brooklyn Dodgers, and singled off Hall of Famer Robin Roberts at Shibe Park for his first major league hit.

He finished the season with Ft. Worth, first place finishers in the Texas League. The following year he played briefly for St. Paul, Minnesota, in the American Association before returning to the Dodgers.

He also played for the Cincinnati Reds ('52), Pittsburgh Pirates ('53-54), Baltimore Orioles ('54-55) and the Chicago White Sox ('56).

In '53 he had his most productive year, appearing in 119 games, collecting 128 hits, belting 15 home runs and ending the season with a .286 batting average.

Cal spent 4 years with the Dodgers on his way to an 8-year pro career.

When the White Sox acquired Larry Doby in '56, Cal was sent to Miami in the International League, where he finished the season and retired.

Of his career in baseball, Cal pleasantly recalls:

"Signing my first professional baseball contract for $75 per month.

"And the day I put on my first Dodgers uniform."

Cal, who is married to May Thaler and has four children and one grandchild, had a heart attack at age 50 and several years ago a quadruple bypass operation.

Yet that doesn't hold back the man who says, "But for the Grace of God, it could have been great."

ANSWERS

487. ▶ Ray Schalk. On August 19, 1919, Mayer was the winning pitcher, as the Chicago White Sox defeated the Philadelphia Athletics, at Comiskey Park, 8-7. Walt Kinney took the loss.

488. ▶ Los Angeles Memorial Coliseum. On July 23, 1959, *Sherry* allowed 7 hits and 3 runs in 7⅓ innings and was relieved by Don Drysdale. The Los Angeles Dodgers defeated the Chicago Cubs, 5-3. Moe Drabowsky was the losing pitcher.

489. ▶ Harvey Kuenn.

490. ▶ Tommy Bridges. On April 18, 1931, in the fourth inning, the St. Louis Browns shortstop hit a 2-run homer. Lefty Stewart yielded 8 hits, as the Browns defeated the Detroit Tigers, at Sportsman's Park, 7-3. *Levey* had 4 runs batted in.

491. ▶ *Benny Kauff.* On September 28, 1916, in the third inning of the second game of a doubleheader, outfielder *Kauff* homered off Pat Ragan. Ferdie Schupp yielded only a seventh-inning single to Ed Konetchy, as the New York Giants defeated the Boston Braves, at the Polo Grounds, 6-0.

492. ▶ *Robert Slater.*

HALL
OF
FAME

493. ▶ In his debut, this Hall of Famer, nick-named "The Old Professor," was caught stealing by Pirates catcher *Mike Simon*...?

ALL-STARS

494. ▶ In 1950, this Phillies MVP surrendered *Sid Gordon*'s fourth grand slam home run of the season...?

1960-
PRESENT

495. ▶ In 1969, this Mets outfielder batted .340 and scored on *Art Shamsky*'s only run-batted-in of the Championship Series...?

1930-59

496. ▶ *Morrie Aderholt* homered in his first major league game in this Washington stadium...?

OLD-TIMERS
1857-1929

497. ▶ In 1905, this Browns Jewish outfielder made an unassisted double play...?

BASEBALL
MISCELLANY

498. ▶ *Greenberg* Gardens was located in this stadium...?

     (Answers next page.)

ANSWERS

493. ► Casey Stengel. On September 17, 1912, the Brooklyn Dodgers center fielder debuted and had 4 hits and a walk. In the second inning, he singled and was caught stealing. Stengel had 2 stolen bases later in the game. Nap Rucker yielded 8 hits, as the Dodgers defeated the Pittsburgh Pirates, at Washington Park, 7-3. Claude Hendrix took the loss. *Simon* had 2 hits, including a double.

494. ► Jim Konstanty. On July 4, 1950, in the ninth inning of the second game of a doubleheader, the Boston Braves left fielder homered. Bobby Hogue was the winning pitcher, as the Braves defeated the Philadelphia Phillies, at Shibe Park, 12-9. Konstanty was the National League's MVP for the 1950 season.

495. ► Cleon Jones. On October 5, 1969, in the second inning of the second game, Jones doubled and scored on *Shamsky's* single off Ron Reed. Reliever Ron Taylor was the winning pitcher, as the New York Mets defeated the Atlanta Braves, at Atlanta Stadium, 11-6. *Shamsky* had 7 hits and a .538 batting average in the Championship Series.

496. ► Griffith Stadium. On September 13, 1939, in the second game of a doubleheader, the Washington Senators second baseman singled and hit a solo home run in his debut. Jack Knott yielded 7 hits, as the Chicago White Sox defeated the Senators, 4-2. Early Wynn was the losing pitcher in a game called after 8 innings.

497. ► *George Stone.*

498. ► Forbes Field, Pittsburgh.

HALL
OF
FAME

499. ► In a 1958 game, Curt Flood and Gene Freese led-off with consecutive home runs off this Jewish Hall of Famer...?

ALL-STARS

500. ► In 1940, *Morrie Arnovich* made his only World Series appearance in this Detroit stadium...?

1960-
PRESENT

501. ► In 1971, this Jewish hurler was traded by the Chicago Cubs to the Oakland Athletics for Rick Monday...?

1930-59

502. ► Indians third baseman *Ralph Winegarner* debuted in 1930 and had his first hit in this stadium...?

OLD-TIMERS
1857-1929

503. ► In 1908, "no-hit" pitcher Johnny Lush yielded a grand slam home run to this Jewish catcher...?

BASEBALL
MISCELLANY

504. ► He is the Jewish author of the baseball story *Rickey and Robinson.*

(Answers next page.)

ANSWERS

499. ► *Sandy Koufax.* On August 17, 1958, in the first game of a doubleheader, the St. Louis Cardinals scored 4 runs in the first inning off *Koufax.* Reliever Jim Brosnan was the winning pitcher, as the Cardinals defeated the Los Angeles Dodgers, at the Memorial Coliseum, 12-7.

ALL-STARS

500. ► Briggs Stadium. On October 5, 1940, in the seventh inning of the fourth game, *Arnovich* batted for Cincinnati Reds left fielder Jimmy Ripple, and was retired by pitcher Archie McKain on a fly ball to right field. *Arnovich* , who replaced Ripple in left field, sacrificed Frank McCormick to second base in the ninth inning. Paul Derringer yielded 5 hits, as the Reds defeated the Detroit Tigers, 5-2. Dizzy Trout took the loss. Pete Fox flied out to Arnovich for the final out of the game.

1930-59

502. ► League Park, Cleveland. On September 20, 1930, the Cleveland Indians third baseman debuted and had 1 hit in 5 at-bats. Milt Gaston yielded 12 hits, as the Boston Red Sox defeated the Indians, 10-3. Roxie Lawson was the losing pitcher. Indians shortstop *Jonah Goldman* had 2 hits.

OLD-TIMERS
1857-1929

503. ► *Johnny Kling.* On September 12, 1908, in the twelfth inning, the Chicago Cubs catcher hit a grand slam homer. Reliever *Ed Reulbach* was the winning pitcher, as the Cubs defeated the St. Louis Cardinals, at Robison Field, 7-3. Lush hurled a no-hitter in 1906, and a 6-inning no-hitter in 1908.

BASEBALL
MISCELLANY

504. ► *Harvey Frommer.*

HALL
OF
FAME

505. ► In his 1948 major league debut, *Marv Rotblatt* surrendered only 1 hit, a single to this Tigers Hall of Famer . . . ?

ALL-STARS

506. ► In 1934, Ralph Birkofer surrendered this Jewish catcher's first major league hit . . . ?

1960-
PRESENT

507. ► *Steve Stone* made his major league debut in this stadium in Southern California . . . ?

1930-59

508. ► In 1936, Greek George was behind the plate for this Indians Jewish player in his only game as a pitcher . . . ?

OLD-TIMERS
1857-1929

509. ► In 1913, this Jewish hurler was traded by the Chicago Cubs to the Brooklyn Dodgers . . . ?

BASEBALL
MISCELLANY

510. ► Jewish athlete *Ed Wineapple* and athletes Gene Conley and Dick Ricketts have this in common . . . ?

       (Answers next page.)

ANSWERS

HALL
OF
FAME

505. ► George Kell. On July 4, 1948, in the first game of a doubleheader, the Chicago White Sox rookie hurled 2 scoreless innings and allowed 1 hit. But Virgil Trucks was the winning pitcher, as the Detroit Tigers defeated the White Sox, at Comiskey Park, 6-3. Bill Wight took the loss.

ALL-STARS

506. ► *Harry Danning.* On May 5, 1934, in the fifth inning, *Danning* batted for pitcher Freddie Fitzsimmons and singled. Birkofer yielded 7 hits, as the Pittsburgh Pirates defeated the New York Giants, at Forbes Field, 6-3.

1960-
PRESENT

507. ► San Diego Stadium. On April 8, 1971, Stone, the San Francisco Giants rookie allowed 6 hits and 4 runs in 3 innings before being relieved. Gary Ross won his only game of the season, as the San Diego Padres defeated the Giants, 7-6. Don McMahon took the loss.

1930-59

508. ► *Milt Galatzer.* On August 26, 1936, the Cleveland Indians outfielder hurled the final 6 innings and allowed 3 runs on 7 hits. Joe Cascarella yielded 5 hits, as the Washington Senators defeated the Indians, at Griffith Stadium, 14-1. Denny Galehouse was the losing pitcher. *Galatzer* had the Indians only RBI.

OLD-TIMERS
1857-1929

509. ► *Ed Reulbach.*

BASEBALL
MISCELLANY

510. ► They played professional baseball and basketball.

HALL
OF
FAME

511. ► In 1902, pitcher *Ham Iburg* made his major league debut as a pinch-hitter against this Giants Hall of Famer...?

ALL-STARS

512. ► *Goody Rosen* scored 126 runs in 1945 and finished second to this teammate, nicknamed "The Brat"...?

1960-
PRESENT

513. ► In a 1977 game, Twins Jewish first baseman *Rod Carew* scored 5 runs in this stadium...?

1930-59

514. ► This noted Giants Jewish slugger hit 2 home runs in 1 inning...?

OLD-TIMERS
1857-1929

515. ► In 1929, *Buddy Myer* had 8 consecutive hits and his streak was stopped in this New York stadium...?

BASEBALL
MISCELLANY

516. ► Who is the author of *The Best Seat In Baseball But You Have To Stand*?

(Answers on page 230.)

BLOCK WANTED TO PLAY BASEBALL

It was the Spring of 1936. In his senior year in Brooklyn's Boys High School, *Cy Block* was making his final attempt to make the baseball team.

Up to then, each year he had been cut. The spring of '36 had been no exception.

"I was heartbroken," he recalls. "All I ever wanted to do was to play baseball."

Cy Block was born May 4, 1919, to Abraham, who emigrated from Dzialoszyce, Poland, and Jenny, who emigrated from Warsaw, Poland.

After graduation in 1936, he tried out with the Brooklyn Dodgers. As was the case in high school, he was cut.

Two years later, he made the long trek down to Orlando, Florida, where he enrolled in Joe Stripp's Baseball School. Some of the hard work showed in the new skills he demonstrated around the field and instructor Joe Tinker was impressed enough to suggest a tryout with the Memphis Chicks of the Southern Association.

Not only did he make it—he was signed to a contract with Paragould in the Northeast Arkansas League—he played regularly at second base and finished the season with a .322 average, setting a league record with 34 stolen bases.

The next season he was a third baseman with Greenville, Mississippi, in the Cotton States League, batting .320.

He persevered through the next 2 seasons with Macon, Georgia, in the South Atlantic League: .313 and a league-leading .357 average.

He also led the league with 109 RBI and was voted Most Valuable Player (1941).

He joined Tulsa in the Texas League (.276 average), and at the end of the 1942 season was promoted to the Chicago Cubs. He took part in 9 games, collected 12 hits, and batted .364.

He enlisted in the Coast Guard as part of the war effort.

Then a little luck entered his hard-working life. Because so many ballplayers were in the military, the league decided that returning servicemen could take part in the World Series.

Cy was back ('45). He had dressed for 2 games. He was in the Series.

Maybe a little rusty from so much baseball inaction, he didn't get to bat, but he was used as a pinch-runner.

For the next 5 years he performed well: .351 in '46 with Nashville in the Southern Association and 6 more games with the Cubs; .363 and a league record 50 doubles with Nashville; .272 and .258 with Buffalo in the International League, and .302 in his

A boy who couldn't make his high school baseball team, as a man *Cy Block* appeared in the World Series as a Chicago Cub.

final year (1950).

He should have had a better shot at the majors.

"Based on my record, I should have gotten a shot, which I never [fully] did," says Cy, who has been in the insurance business since 1948.

Still, Cy Block, husband of Harriet Spektor and father of three girls, has the last laugh.

He's still making money from baseball, and giving it all to charity through the sale of his book, *So You Want To Be a Major Leaguer?*

ANSWERS

511. ► Christy Mathewson. On April 17, 1902, *Iburg* debuted on Opening Day when he batted for reliever Cy Vorhees in the ninth inning. Mathewson yielded 4 hits, as the New York Giants defeated the Philadelphia Phillies, at the Polo Grounds, 7-0. Harry Felix took the loss.

512. ► Eddie Stanky. On September 30, 1945, the Brooklyn Dodgers second baseman scored his 128th run of the season while *Rosen* was held hitless and failed to score. Hal Gregg was the winning pitcher, as the Dodgers defeated the Philadelphia Phillies, at Shibe Park, 4-1. Hugh Mulcahy took the loss.

513. ► Metropolitan Stadium, Bloomington. On June 26, 1977, the Minnesota Twins first baseman had his sixth 4-hit game of the season. *Carew* had a home run, double, 2 singles, 6 runs-batted-in and scored 5 runs. Reliever Tom Johnson was the winning pitcher, as the Twins defeated the Chicago White Sox, 19-12. *Steve Stone* was the losing pitcher.

514. ► *Sid Gordon.*

515. ► Yankee Stadium. On August 6, 1929, the Washington Senators second baseman had 4 hits, including 3 doubles, 3 runs scored and 3 RBI before being retired. Bump Hadley was the winning pitcher, as the Senators defeated the New York Yankees, 13-9. Ed Wells took the loss. In the previous game, *Myer* had 4 hits, including a home run, 4 runs scored and 7 RBI.

516. ► *Lee Gutkind.*

HALL
OF
FAME

517. ► In 1955, this Pirates Hall of Famer was the first player to score a run off *Sandy Koufax,* the National League ERA leader, 1962-1966. . . ?

ALL-STARS

518. ► In 1976, this Reds lefthander surrendered *Elliott Maddox'* only World Series hit and later signed as a free agent with the New York Yankees. . . ?

1960-
PRESENT

519. ► Billy O'Dell surrendered this Jewish catcher's 107th and last major league hit in 1963. . . ?

1930-59

520. ► Rookie *Morrie Arnovich's* home run enabled the Philadelphia Phillies to win their 1937 season opener in this Boston stadium. . . ?

OLD-TIMERS
1857-1929

521. ► This Cubs Jewish catcher was behind the plate in the 1908 pennant-winning game against the New York Giants. . . ?

BASEBALL
MISCELLANY

522. ► *Al Forman* was an umpire when this Braves Hall of Famer won his 290th victory and hurled his second no-hitter. . . ?

(Answers next page.)

ANSWERS

517. ► Roberto Clemente. On July 6, 1955, in the fifth inning of the second game of a doubleheader, Clemente scored on a bases-loaded walk to Dale Long by the Brooklyn Dodgers rookie. Vernon Law yielded 9 hits, as the Pittsburgh Pirates defeated the Dodgers, at Forbes Field, 4-1. Ed Roebuck was the losing pitcher.

518. ► Don Gullett. On October 16, 1976, in the fifth inning of the first game, Maddox, the New York Yankees right fielder, tripled. Gullett, with relief help from Pedro Borbon, was the winning pitcher, as the Cincinnati Reds defeated the Yankees, at Riverfront Stadium, 5-1. Doyle Alexander took the loss.

519. ► *Norm Sherry.* On September 21, 1963, in the fourth inning, the New York Mets catcher singled to score Chico Fernandez. Al Jackson was the winning pitcher, as the Mets defeated the San Francisco Giants, at Candlestick Park, 5-4.

520. ► Braves Field. On April 19, 1937, in the eleventh inning, the rookie left fielder homered off Guy Bush. Reliever Wayne LaMaster debuted and was the winning pitcher. The Philadelphia Phillies defeated the Boston Bees, in the morning game, 2-1. Bucky Walters yielded 4 hits, as the Phillies won the afternoon game, 1-0.

521. ► *Johnny Kling.*

522. ► Warren Spahn. April 28, 1961, when the Braves blanked San Francisco, 1-0.

523. ► This Giants Hall of Famer, nicknamed "Say Hey," was the first player to hit a home run off pitcher *Ed Mayer*...?

524. ► In 1949, this Jewish hurler, a future ERA leader, was the losing pitcher in his debut...?

525. ► Duane Kuiper hit his only home run in 3,379 at-bats (1974-1985) off this Jewish Cy Young Award winner...?

526. ► In 1943, Phillies pitcher *Dick Conger* had his only major league hit in this stadium...?

527. ► In 1916, this Jewish outfielder contributed 2 singles, 2 stolen bases and scored 1 run in the New York Giants' twenty-sixth consecutive victory of the season...?

528. ► He is the Jewish author of *The South Paw*...?

ANSWERS

523. ► Willie Mays. On September 15, 1957, in the second game of a doubleheader, *Mayer*, the Chicago Cubs hurler, debuted and allowed 5 runs in 5 innings. Reliever Don Elston was the winning pitcher, as the Cubs defeated the New York Giants, at Wrigley Field, 7-6. Stu Miller took the loss. Mayer singled off Giants starter Mike McCormick.

524. ► *Saul Rogovin.* On April 28, 1949, *Rogovin* relieved Ted Gray and allowed 3 runs on 4 hits in 1⅓ innings. Bob Malloy was the winning pitcher, as the St. Louis Browns defeated the Detroit Tigers, at Briggs Stadium, 9-6. Two years later Rogovin led the American League with a 2.78 ERA.

525. ► *Steve Stone.* On August 29, 1977, in the first inning, the Cleveland Indians second baseman homered on his 1,382nd at-bat. Rick Waits yielded 6 hits, as the Indians defeated the Chicago White Sox, at Municipal Stadium, 9-2.

526. ► Shibe Park, Philadelphia. On August 17, 1943, the Philadelphia Phillies hurler had a single in 3 at-bats. Ray Prim, who relieved Hank Wyse in the seventh inning, was the winning pitcher, as the Chicago Cubs defeated the Phillies, 7-5.

527. ► *Benny Kauff.*

528. ► *Mark Harris.*

529. ► This Jewish Hall of Famer had 3 strike-outs in an inning on 9 pitches twice in his career...?

530. ► Nicknamed "Muddy," he caught Walter Johnson's first World Series victory as well as pitcher *Izzy Goldstein* in his debut...?

531. ► Frank Viola surrendered this Jewish Angels' 3,000th career hit...?

532. ► Catcher *Chick Starr* debuted in this Chicago stadium...?

533. ► In 1916, Jewish player *Sammy Bohne* debuted at shortstop for the Cardinals playing between these Hall of Famers, nicknamed "Rajah" and "The Mighty Mite"...?

534. ► What do Elizabeth Taylor and baseball's Elliott Maddox have in common...?

(Answers next page.)

ANSWERS

529. ▶ *Sandy Koufax.* He performed this feat on June 30, 1962 and April 18, 1964.

530. ▶ Muddy Ruel. On April 24, 1932, in the second inning, *Goldstein* debuted in relief for the Detroit Tigers and allowed 1 run in 1 inning. Art Herring was the winning pitcher, as the Tigers defeated the Chicago White Sox, at Navin Field, 10-9. Red Faber took the loss.

531. ▶ *Rod Carew.* On August 4, 1985, in the third inning, the California Angels first baseman singled. Stu Cliburn was the winning pitcher, as the Angels defeated the Minnesota Twins, at Anaheim Stadium, 6-5. Frank Eufemia took the loss.

532. ▶ Comiskey Park. On August 23, 1935, in the tenth inning, John Stone pinch-hit for Sammy Holbrook and walked to force in Heinie Manush with the winning run. *Starr* replaced Holbrook as the Washington Senators catcher. He caught Jack Russell's pitches as the Senators defeated the Chicago White Sox, 4-3. Les Tietje took the loss.

533. ▶ Rogers Hornsby, third base, and Miller Huggins, second base. On September 9, 1916, in the first game of a doubleheader, Bohne pinch-hit and then played shortstop in the tenth inning when the Cincinnati Reds scored 3 runs. Al Schulz yielded 9 hits, as the Reds defeated the St. Louis Cardinals, at Robison Field, 6-3. Steamboat Williams took the loss.

534. ▶ They are converts to Judaism.

535. ► *Phil Weintraub* played in the 1945 game in which this Giants Hall of Famer hit his 500th career home run...?

536. ► In a 1939 game, *Morrie Arnovich* had 5 hits in this Pittsburgh stadium...?

537. ► *Art Shamsky* debuted against this Cardinals Hall of Fame hurler...?

538. ► In 1932, Glenn Myatt caught *Ralph Winegarner*'s first career victory in which Cleveland stadium...?

539. ► Giants center fielder *Benny Kauff* fanned 30 times during the 1918 season, including 5 strikeouts in 1 game in this St. Louis stadium...?

540. ► The Jewish author of *Baseball's Greatest Moments* is...?

(Answers on page 240.)

I COULD HAVE BEEN A CONTENDER

"The game of baseball is great, but I disliked the business of baseball," says *Mickey Rutner*.

"Several times during my career, I felt that I was ready for the majors."

His record certainly indicates high potential.

Twelve hits, 12 games, 48 at-bats with 4 RBI and 1 homer—when he was given a chance to play in the majors. His record in the minor leagues was even more impressive.

"Although I never won a batting title or a home run crown, I almost always made the All-Star team in whatever league I was playing in."

The third-baseman's first All-Star rating occurred in 1942, his sophomore year in professional baseball, when he suited up for Wilmington, Delaware, in the Inter-State League. The previous year he had played with Winston-Salem, North Carolina, in the Piedmont League.

On the second team was George Kell, who played for Lancaster and later was a Hall of Famer.

His second All-Star ranking occurred after a 2-year stint with the 45th Division in Europe during the war ('42-45), as a member of Wilmington's squad.

He had batted .350 and had over 100 RBI.

Following a year with Birmingham, Alabama, of the Southern Association, came his shot at the majors with the Philadelphia Athletics.

"I appeared in 12 games," he said from the Town of Hempstead, New York, where since '74 he has been the Supervisor of Recreation.

Manager Connie Mack put him in against Joe Haynes of the Chicago White Sox, and he went 2 for 4. In one of those games he homered against Earl Caldwell of the White Sox.

"In my first game at Yankee Stadium, with the likes of Joe DiMaggio and Phil Rizzuto in the game, I blasted a hit against Joe Page that won the game."

So why then didn't he make it to the top?

The businessmen in the front office decided they didn't need the services of New York-born Mickey Rutner, the youngest of 5 children born to Max and Rose who were immigrants from Lodz in Poland.

"I don't know why," he said. "In 48 at bats, I had 12 hits including 1 double, 1 home run, 4 RBI and a .250 batting average."

Following the 1947 season, Mickey was offered an unimpressive contract by Connie Mack that was at a lower salary than he had previously earned with Birmingham.

"I had no choice but to sign," he now recalls.

Mack gave him a tryout in

Mickey Rutner, with manager Connie Mack, prepares for a game in Philadelphia Athletics uniform.

spring training, then shipped him off to play for Birmingham.

He was again on the All-Star team, and his team won the Dixie Series, defeating Ft. Worth of the Texas League.

His hopes of impressing the front-office businessmen soared the next year when the Boston Red Sox picked up his contract.

But instead of giving him a shot at the majors, they sent him to Louisville in the American Association. Later that season he played for Tulsa and took part in the Texas League play-offs.

He rounded out his career, still in the minors, with Toronto of the International League, where he batted close to .300.

The next year he spent with San Antonio. Again he was on the Texas League All-Star team.

But despite all this, there was still no offer from the majors.

His final 2 seasons were spent with Tulsa and Oklahoma City in the Texas League.

In '41 Mickey married Leona Schiff, a dancer with the Rock-ettes. They have three sons: Toby, a psychologist in Winnipeg, Manitoba, Canada, Richard, an artist in New York City, and Paul, a musician in California.

Today he still believes that he was ready for the majors. Who knows? Maybe he was. He could have been a contender.

ANSWERS

HALL
OF
FAME

535. ▶ Mel Ott.

ALL-STARS

536. ▶ Forbes Field. On May 17, 1939, the Philadelphia Phillies left fielder had 5 hits, including a double, and scored 2 runs. Hugh Mulcahy yielded 5 hits, as the Phillies defeated the Pittsburgh Pirates, 7-3. Bob Klinger was the losing pitcher.

1960-
PRESENT

537. ▶ Bob Gibson. On April 17, 1965, the Cincinnati Reds pinch-hitter was retired in his only at-bat of the game. Gibson yielded 8 hits, as the St. Louis Cardinals defeated the Reds, at Busch Stadium, 8-0. Jim O'Toole took the loss.

1930-59

538. ▶ Municipal Stadium. On September 25, 1932, in the first game of a doubleheader, *Winegarner* allowed 6 hits and 10 walks in winning his first game. The Cleveland Indians defeated the Chicago White Sox, 6-4. Paul Gregory was the losing pitcher.

OLD-TIMERS
1857-1929

539. ▶ Robison Field. On May 23, 1918, pitchers Jakie May, Bill Doak and Bill Sherdel combined to stop *Kauff,* who had no hits in 7 at-bats. Fred Anderson was the winning pitcher, as the New York Giants defeated the St. Louis Cardinals, in 14 innings, 6-4.

BASEBALL
MISCELLANY

540. ▶ *Joseph L. Reichler.*

HALL
OF
FAME

541. ▶ Cubs hurler Ray Prim surrendered this Jewish slugger's twenty-seventh and last World Series hit...?

ALL-STARS

542. ▶ This "blooper ball" pitcher, nicknamed "Rip," surrendered a grand slam home run to *Harry Danning* in 1938...?

1960-
PRESENT

543. ▶ In 1981, pitcher *Steve Ratzer*'s only major league victory was caught by this Expos All-Star...?

1930-59

544. ▶ Name 2 of the 3 Jewish players on the 1934 Cleveland Indians...?

OLD-TIMERS
1857-1929

545. ▶ *Buddy Myer*, a Senators Jewish rookie, debuted in this stadium...?

BASEBALL
MISCELLANY

546. ▶ This Jewish hurler's uniform number (32) was retired by the Los Angeles Dodgers...?

ANSWERS

541. ▶ *Hank Greenberg.* On October 8, 1945, in the eighth inning of the sixth game, the Detroit Tigers left fielder hit a solo home run to tie the score. Stan Hack's twelfth-inning double scored Bill Schuster to end the game. Hank Borowy was the winning pitcher, as the Chicago Cubs defeated the Tigers, at Wrigley Field, 8-7. Dizzy Trout took the loss. *Greenberg* had 7 doubles, 2 triples, 5 home runs, 22 RBIs and a .318 World Series batting average.

ALL-STARS

542. ▶ Rip Sewell. On May 22, 1938, the New York Giants catcher hit a 2-run triple in the third inning and batted a grand slam homer in the seventh inning. Carl Hubbell yielded 10 hits, as the Giants defeated the Pittsburgh Pirates, at the Polo Grounds, 18-2. Ed Brandt was the losing pitcher.

1960-
PRESENT

543. ▶ Gary Carter. On April 28, 1981, the Montreal Expos rookie hurled a scoreless inning in relief of Charlie Lea. *Ratzer* became the winning pitcher when the Expos scored 2 runs in the sixth inning. The Expos defeated the Philadelphia Phillies, at Veterans Stadium, 6-3. Larry Christenson took the loss.

1930-59

544. ▶ *Moe Berg, Milt Galatzer* and *Ralph Winegarner.*

OLD-TIMERS
1857-1929

545. ▶ Griffith Stadium, Washington. On September 26, 1925, in the ninth inning, *Myer* replaced Everett Scott at shortstop. Elam Vangilder was the winning pitcher, as the St. Louis Browns defeated the Washington Senators, 9-7. Lefty Thomas took the loss.

BASEBALL
MISCELLANY

546. ▶ *Sandy Koufax.*

HALL
OF
FAME

547. ▶ In 1930, *Jimmy Reese* debuted and pinch-hit for this Hall of Famer, who won 240 major league games...?

ALL-STARS

548. ▶ This Jewish hurler was the winner of the 1965 All-Star Game...?

1960-
PRESENT

549. ▶ Al Fitzmorris took the loss when this Angels Jewish pitcher won his eighth and last major league victory...?

1930-59

550. ▶ In 1938, Phillies infielder *Eddie Feinberg* debuted in this stadium...?

OLD-TIMERS
1857-1929

551. ▶ This Jewish hurler, who later entertained millions at baseball games, was the winning pitcher in his debut...?

BASEBALL
MISCELLANY

552. ▶ Who is the Jewish author of the baseball book called *The Seventh Game*?

ANSWERS

HALL
OF
FAME

547. ▶ Herb Pennock. On April 19, 1930, in the eighth inning of the afternoon game, *Reese*, the New York Yankees pinch-hitter, singled and scored. Jack Russell yielded 7 hits, as the Boston Red Sox defeated the Yankees, at Braves Field, 7-2. The Patriots' Day doubleheader was moved to the larger-seating National League stadium.

ALL-STARS

548. ▶ *Sandy Koufax.*

1960-
PRESENT

549. ▶ *Lloyd Allen.* On July 30, 1972, the California Angels reliever hurled 4 innings and allowed 1 run on 4 hits. Bob Oliver's eleventh-inning homer gave *Allen* the victory. The Angels defeated the Kansas City Royals, at Anaheim Stadium, 4-3.

1930-59

550. ▶ Shibe Park, Philadelphia. On September 11, 1938, in the ninth inning of the second game of a doubleheader, *Feinberg* ran for Pinky Whitney. Ira Hutchinson was the winning pitcher, as the Boston Bees defeated the Philadelphia Phillies, 3-2. Max Butcher took the loss.

OLD-TIMERS
1857-1929

531. ▶ *Al Schacht.* On September 18, 1919, in the first game of a doubleheader, *Schacht* yielded 10 hits, as the Washington Senators defeated the St. Louis Browns, at Griffith Stadium, 12-3. Allan Sothoron was the losing pitcher.

BASEBALL
MISCELLANY

552. ▶ *Roger Kahn.*

553. ► *Johnny Kling* debuted in 1900 and caught this Hall of Famer, nicknamed, "The Old Fox"...?

554. ► In a 1969 game, Mickey Lolich and Bill Freehan were the opposing battery when this Twins Jewish star stole second, third and home in the same inning...?

555. ► In 1974, *Richie Scheinblum* had his 320th and last career hit in this Pittsburgh stadium...?

556. ► In 1951, Matt Batts caught for this Parisians Jewish pitcher in his debut...?

557. ► This Giants Jewish outfielder made an unassisted double play in 1916...?

558. ► *Jim Levey,* and athletes Greasy Neale and Tom Yewcic have this in common...?

(Answers next page.)

ANSWERS

HALL
OF
FAME

553. ▶ Clark Griffith. On September 11, 1900, in the second game of a doubleheader at the Polo Grounds, *Kling*, the Chicago Cubs catcher. debuted and had 3 singles. Griffith yielded 6 hits and New York Giants pitcher Bill Carrick allowed 7 hits, as the game was called after nine innings with the score 3-3.

ALL-STARS

554. ▶ *Rod Carew.* On May 18, 1969, in the third inning, Cesar Tovar singled and *Carew* walked. They pulled a double steal followed by Tovar's theft of home. *Carew* then stole third and home. Lolich yielded 4 hits, as the Detroit Tigers defeated the Minnesota Twins, at Metropolitan Stadium, 8-2. Dave Boswell was the losing pitcher. *Carew* led the league with a .332 batting average.

1960-
PRESENT

555. ▶ Three Rivers Stadium. On September 19, 1974, in the eighth inning, the St. Louis Cardinals pinch-hitter singled. Ramon Hernandez was the winning pitcher, as the Pittsburgh Pirates defeated the Cardinals, 8-6. Rich Folkers took the loss.

1930-59

556. ▶ *Duke Markell.* On September 6, 1951, *Markell* debuted and, pitching in relief of Jim McDonald, allowed 1 run on 4 hits in 3 innings. Randy Gumpert yielded 7 hits, as the Chicago White Sox defeated the St. Louis Browns, at Sportsman's Park, 9-4. McDonald was the losing pitcher.

OLD-TIMERS
1857-1929

557. ▶ *Benny Kauff.*

BASEBALL
MISCELLANY

558. ▶ They played professional baseball and football.

559. ▶ This Jewish slugger holds the Detroit Tigers all-time record for most home runs in one season . . . ?

560. ▶ *Al Rosen* hit his first grand slam home run in this Washington stadium . . . ?

561. ▶ Terry Forster was the losing pitcher when this Jewish hurler won his twenty-first and final victory of the 1973 regular season . . . ?

562. ▶ In 1943, Mickey Livingston caught this Phillies Jewish pitcher's first National League victory . . . ?

563. ▶ In the first game at St. Louis' Sportsman's Park, *Lipman Pike* had 1 hit off this White Stockings Hall of Famer who hurled and managed his team to the 1876 pennant . . . ?

564. ▶ The Jewish author of *Baseball's Greatest Rivalry—New York Yankees/ Boston Red Sox* is . . . ?

(Answers next page.)

ANSWERS

559. ▶ *Hank Greenberg* hit 58 home runs in 1938.

560. ▶ Griffith Stadium. On June 8, 1950, in the first inning, the Cleveland Indians third baseman hit a grand slam homer off Bob Kuzava. Reliever Mickey Harris' ninth-inning single scored John Ostrowski with the winning run. The Washington Senators defeated the Indians, 7-6. Gene Bearden was the losing pitcher. *Rosen* had 9 career grand slam homers.

561. ▶ *Ken Holtzman.* On September 29, 1973, *Holtzman* hurled 7 innings and allowed 3 earned runs with 7 strikeouts, as the Oakland Athletics defeated the Chicago White Sox, at the Oakland Coliseum, 7-5.

562. ▶ *Dick Conger.* On July 17, 1943, in the first game of a doubleheader, *Conger* allowed 2 hits, as the Philadelphia Phillies defeated the New York Giants, at Shibe Park, 2-1. Johnnie Wittig took the loss.

563. ▶ Al Spalding. On May 5, 1876, the St. Louis Brown Stockings center fielder had 1 of 7 hits allowed by Spalding. George Bradley yielded 2 hits, as the Brown Stockings defeated the Chicago White Stockings, 1-0.

564. ▶ *Harvey Frommer.*

HALL
OF
FAME

565. ► *Chief Roseman* had 3 hits in the 1884 World Series off this 60-game winner...?

ALL-STARS

566. ► In 1947, which White Sox hurler surrendered Jewish third baseman *Mickey Rutner*'s first major league hit and had the lowest ERA in the league?

1960-
PRESENT

567. ► Name 2 of the 3 Jewish players on the New York Mets 1960-1969...?

1930-59

568. ► In 1936, Jake Wade surrendered this Senators Jewish outfielder's first major league home run...?

OLD-TIMERS
1857-1929

569. ► In a 1918 game, Jewish pitcher *Erskine Mayer* hurled 15⅓ scoreless innings in this Boston stadium...?

BASEBALL
MISCELLANY

570. ► Which Dodger hurler married the daughter of movie actor Richard Widmark?

ANSWERS

565. ► Charles (Hoss) Radbourn. On October 23-25, 1884, Radbourn allowed 2 hits, 3 hits and 6 hits in winning all three games for the Providence Grays over the New York Metropolitans. *Roseman* had a single in the second game and 2 singles in the final game.

566. ► Joe Haynes. On September 11, 1947, *Rutner*, the Philadelphia Athletics third baseman, debuted and had 2 singles in 4 at-bats. The Chicago White Sox defeated the Athletics, at Shibe Park, 7-3. Joe Coleman was the losing pitcher. In 1947 a pitcher could qualify for ERA leader with 10 complete games. Today, only those who pitched 162 innings can qualify. By this rule, Haynes would have won the ERA title.

567. ► *Joe Ginsberg, Art Shamsky* and *Norm Sherry.*

568. ► *Fred Sington.* On September 9, 1936, in the ninth inning, *Sington*, the Washington Senators right fielder, hit a solo home run. Joe Cascarella yielded 10 hits, as the Senators defeated the Detroit Tigers, at Navin Field, 11-4.

569. ► Braves Field. On August 1, 1918, the Pittsburgh Pirates pitcher allowed 12 hits and was relieved in the sixteenth inning by Wilbur Cooper. The Pirates defeated the Boston Braves, in 21 innings, 2-0. Art Nehf yielded 12 hits for the losing Braves.

570. ► *Sandy Koufax.*

Baseball Judaica QUESTIONS

HALL
OF
FAME
571. ▶ *Hank Greenberg* scored 5 runs in 1 game in this Philadelphia park...?

ALL-STARS
572. ▶ This Expo hurled 2 no-hitters and was the opposing pitcher when outfielder *Richie Scheinblum* had his only at-bat in an All-Star Game...?

1960-
PRESENT
573. ▶ In 1960, this pitcher, who would soon be traded and hurl a no-hitter, won the only game managed by *Andy Cohen*...?

1930-59
574. ▶ Name 3 of the 4 Jewish players on the 1934 Washington Senators...?

OLD-TIMERS
1857-1929
575. ▶ In 1916, Lefty Tyler was the opposing pitcher when this Jewish former Federal League stolen base champion was caught off first base 3 times in 1 game...?

BASEBALL
MISCELLANY
576. ▶ Who is the author of *Baseball's 100*?

(Answers next page.)

ANSWERS

571. ▶ Shibe Park. On July 30, 1939, in the first game of a doubleheader, *Greenberg*, the Detroit Tigers first baseman, had 4 hits, including a home run and a double. Bobo Newsom yielded 5 hits, as the Tigers defeated the Philadelphia Athletics, 14-0. Bill Beckman was the losing pitcher.

572. ▶ Bill Stoneman. On July 25, 1972, *Scheinblum* of the Kansas City Royals entered the game as a replacement in right field, and in the eighth inning grounded out in his only at bat. Joe Morgan's tenth-inning single scored Nate Colbert to end the game. Tug McGraw was the winning pitcher, as the National League defeated the American League, at Atlanta Stadium, 4-3. Dave McNally took the loss.

573. ▶ Don Cardwell. On April 14, 1960, *Cohen* managed the Philadelphia Phillies until the arrival of Gene Mauch. In the tenth inning, Joe Koppe's single scored Bobby Del Greco with the winning run. The Phillies defeated the Milwaukee Braves, at Connie Mack Stadium, 5-4. Juan Pizzaro was the losing pitcher.

574. ▶ *Moe Berg, Syd Cohen, Buddy Myer* and *Fred Sington.*

575. ▶ *Benny Kauff.* On May 26, 1916, the New York Giants center fielder had no hits in 2 at bats and scored 1 run. Sailor Stroud was the winning pitcher, as the Giants defeated the Boston Braves, at Braves Field, 12-1.

576. ▶ *Maury Allen.*

577. ► In 1960, this Hall of Fame knuckleballer was pitching when *Joe Ginsberg* had 3 passed balls in 1 inning...?

578. ► In 1946, Jewish star *Goody Rosen* was traded by the Brooklyn Dodgers to the New York Giants and on the first day for his new team had 5 hits in a double-header in this stadium...?

579. ► This New York Mets Jewish batter had his only pinch-hit of the 1968 season off Reds hurler Jay Ritchie...?

580. ► Shortstop *Lou Brower* had his first major league hit in this New York stadium...?

581. ► *Johnny Kling*, in his only successful pinch-hitting appearance of the 1911 season, batted for this Hall of Famer for whom a pitching award is named...?

582. ► Cut by the Dodgers (1955) to make room on the roster for *Sandy Koufax*, he became the Los Angeles manager in 1976...?

(Answers next page.)

ANSWERS

577. ► Hoyt Wilhelm. On May 10, 1960, in the second inning, *Ginsberg,* the Baltimore Orioles catcher, tied an American League record with 3 passed balls. Dick Hall yielded 6 hits, as the Kansas City Athletics defeated the Orioles, at Memorial Stadium, 10-0.

578. ► Polo Grounds, New York. On April 28, 1946, in the first game, *Rosen* had 3 singles and scored 2 runs. Hal Schumacher yielded 7 hits, as the New York Giants defeated the Brooklyn Dodgers, 7-3. Joe Hatten was the losing pitcher. In the second game, *Rosen* had 2 hits, including a home run, 3 RBI and scored 2 runs. Bob Joyce allowed 10 hits, as the Giants defeated the Dodgers, 10-4. Hank Behrman took the loss.

579. ► *Art Shamsky.* On August 24, 1968, in the seventh inning, *Shamsky* batted for reliever Cal Koonce and hit a 2-run homer. Jerry Arrigo was the winning pitcher, as the Cincinnati Reds defeated the New York Mets, at Crosley Field, 10-7. Jerry Koosman took the loss.

580. ► Yankee Stadium. On June 15, 1931, the Detroit Tigers shortstop had a single and scored 2 runs. Earl Whitehill was the winning pitcher, as the Tigers defeated the New York Yankees, 8-5. Red Ruffing took the loss.

581. ► Cy Young. On September 30, 1911, in the ninth inning of the second game of a doubleheader, *Kling* singled off Rube Benton. Benton yielded 10 hits, as the Cincinnati Reds defeated the Boston Pilgrims, at Redland Field, 4-1. This was Young's last complete game. Annually, the Cy Young Award is presented to the major leagues' top pitcher.

582. ► Tom LaSorda.

HALL
OF
FAME

583. ► Which Hall of Famer was the first National League hurler to fan 300 batters in one season?

ALL-STARS

584. ► Shortstop *Al Richter* had his only major league hit off this Yankees hurler, the winner of the 1947 All-Star Game...?

1960-
PRESENT

585. ► Name 2 of the 3 Jewish players on the 1961 Los Angeles Dodgers...?

1930-59

586. ► In 1945, Dick Barrett surrendered this Giants Jewish first baseman's 407th and last major league hit...?

OLD-TIMERS
1857-1929

587. ► Senators Jewish outfielder *Sam Mayer* suited up for his first game in this stadium...?

BASEBALL
MISCELLANY

588. ► He authored the well-known *Fabulous Baseball Facts, Feats and Figures*...?

ANSWERS

583. ► *Sandy Koufax* had 306 strikeouts in 1963.

584. ► Spec Shea. On September 30, 1951, on the final day of the season, the Boston Red Sox shortstop had a single in 4 at-bats. Shea, with relief help from Johnny Sain, was the winning pitcher, as the New York Yankees defeated the Red Sox, at Yankee Stadium, 3-0. Harley Hisner appeared in his only major league game and took the loss.

585. ► *Sandy Koufax, Larry Sherry* and *Norm Sherry.* That season they finished in second place with 89 wins and 65 losses.

586. ► *Phil Weintraub.* On August 5, 1945, in the second game of a doubleheader at the Polo Grounds, the New York Giants first baseman singled off the Phillies hurler. Ace Adams was the winning pitcher, as the Giants defeated the Philadelphia Phillies, in 13 innings, 4-2. Andy Karl took the loss.

587. ► Griffith Stadium, Washington. On September 4, 1915, the Washington Senators right fielder had no hits in 4 at-bats. Bert Gallia was the winning pitcher, as the Senators defeated the New York Yankees, 4-3. Reliever George Mogridge took the loss.

588. ► *Joseph L. Reichler.*

HALL
OF
FAME

589. ► This Reds hurler, nicknamed "Junior," surrendered *Hank Greenberg*'s only home run in the 1940 World Series...?

ALL-STARS

590. ► Giants catcher *Harry Danning* (1933-1942) played his last major league game in this historic stadium...?

1960-
PRESENT

591. ► Player *Steve Ratzer* lost his only major league game to this 1981 Cy Young Award winner and Rookie of the Year...?

1930-59

592. ► In 1932, this hurler, nicknamed "Jumbo Jim," surrendered outfielder *Max Rosenfeld*'s first career home run...?

OLD-TIMERS
1857-1929

593. ► Name 2 of the 3 Jewish players on John McGraw's New York Giants between 1920 and 1929?

BASEBALL
MISCELLANY

594. ► This pitcher missed his starting assignment in the 1965 World Series to attend religious services...?

       (Answers next page.)

ANSWERS

589. ► Junior Thompson. On October 6, 1940, in the third inning of the fifth game, Greenberg's homer scored Barney McCosky and Charlie Gehringer. Bobo Newsom yielded 3 hits, as the Detroit Tigers defeated the Cincinnati Reds, at Briggs Stadium, 8-0. In 1940, *Greenberg* led the American League in home runs and runs batted in.

590. ► Polo Grounds, New York. On September 25, 1942, in the second game of a doubleheader, *Danning* singled and scored the New York Giants' only run. Si Johnson yielded 6 hits, as the Philadelphia Phillies defeated the Giants, 9-1. Outfielder Hank Leiber made his only appearance as a pitcher and took the loss.

591. ► Fernando Valenzuela. On May 14, 1981, Pedro Guerrero led off the ninth inning with a home run off the Expos reliever. Valenzuela yielded 3 hits, as the Los Angeles Dodgers defeated the Montreal Expos, at Dodger Stadium, 3-2.

592. ► Jim Elliott. On April 28, 1932, in the eighth inning, the Brooklyn Robins right fielder hit a 3-run homer. Ray Phelps allowed 10 hits, as the Robins defeated the Philadelphia Phillies, at Baker Bowl, 11-5. Ed Holley was the losing pitcher.

593. ► *Andy Cohen, Benny Kauff* and *Moe Solomon.*

594. ► *Sandy Koufax.*

HALL
OF
FAME

595. ► This Jewish slugger hit 2 home runs in a game 35 times...?

ALL-STARS

596. ► In 1959, catcher *Joe Ginsberg* was behind the plate when this Indian hit his fourth home run of the game...?

1960-
PRESENT

597. ► In 1961, pitcher *Howie Koplitz* debuted in this Boston stadium...?

1930-59

598. ► New York Giants first baseman *Mike Schemer* debuted in which stadium...?

OLD-TIMERS
1857-1929

599. ► This Cubs player caught the play-off of the tie game that settled the 1908 pennant race...?

BASEBALL
MISCELLANY

600. ► Signed during his freshman year at the University of Cincinnati, he pitched for the Dodgers and is in the Hall of Fame...?

ANSWERS

595. ► *Hank Greenberg.*

596. ► Rocky Colavito. On June 10, 1959, in the ninth inning, Colavito, the Cleveland Indians right fielder, hit a solo homer off Ernie Johnson, his fourth of the   game. Gary Bell was the winning pitcher, as the Indians defeated the Baltimore Orioles, at Memorial Stadium, 11-8. Jerry Walker took the loss.

597. ► Fenway Park. On September 8, 1961, Koplitz, the Detroit Tigers rookie, hurled a scoreless eighth inning, allowing 1 hit. Reliever Mike Fornieles was the winning pitcher, as the Boston Red Sox defeated the Tigers, 9-2. Jim Bunning took the loss.

598. ► Polo Grounds, New York. On August 8, 1945, the New York Giants rookie had 2 singles in 4 at-bats. George Dockins yielded 6 hits, as the St. Louis Cardinals defeated the Giants, 3-0. Van Lingle Mungo was the losing pitcher.

599. ► *Johnny Kling.* On October 8, 1908, the Chicago Cubs catcher singled and scored in the 4-run third inning. Three Finger Brown was the winning pitcher, as the Cubs defeated the New York Giants, at the Polo Grounds, 4-2. Christy Mathewson took the loss.

600. ► *Sandy Koufax.*

STATISTICS

JEWISH PROFESSIONAL BASEBALL PLAYERS

ABBREVIATIONS

Leagues

A — American League
AA — American Association
F — Federal League
NA — National Association
N — National League
P — Players' League
UA — Union Association

Positions

1B — First Base
2B — Second Base
SS — Shortstop
3B — Third Base
INF — 1B, 2B, SS and 3B (Infield)
OF — Outfield
C — Catcher
P — Pitcher
MGR — Manager

Statistics

G — Games
AB — At Bats
R — Runs
H — Hits
HR — Home Runs
RBI — Runs-Batted-In
AVG — Batting Average
IP — Innings Pitched
SO — Strikeouts
BB — Bases on Balls
W — Wins
L — Losses
ERA — Earned Run Average

Batters		G	AB	R	H	HR	RBI	AVG
Cal Abrams (1924-) Brooklyn (1949-52) Cincinnati (1952) Pittsburgh (1953-54) Baltimore (1954-55) Chicago (A) (1956)	OF-1B	567	1611	257	433	32	138	.269
Morrie Aderholt (1915-55) Washington (1939-41) Brooklyn (1944-45) Boston (N) (1945)	2B-3B OF	106	262	36	70	3	32	.267
Morrie Arnovich (1910-59) Philadelphia (N) (1936-40) Cincinnati (1940) New York (N) (1941, '46)	OF	590	2013	234	577	22	261	.287
Jake Atz (1879-1945) Washington (1902) Chicago (A) (1907-09)	2B-SS 3B-OF	208	604	64	132	0	49	.219
Steve Behel (1860-1945) Milwaukee (UA) (1884) New York (AA) (1886)	OF	68	257	37	54	0	NA	.210
Joe Bennett (1900-) Philadelphia (N) (1923)	3B	1	0	0	0	0	0	
Moe Berg (1902-72) Brooklyn (1923) Chicago (A) (1926-30) Cleveland (1931, 1934) Washington (1932-34) Boston (A) (1935-39)	C-INF	662	1812	150	441	6	206	.243
Nate Berkenstock (1831-1900) Philadelphia (NA) (1871)	OF	1	4	0	0	0		.000
Bob Berman (1899-) Washington (1918)	C	2	0	0	0	0	0	
Cy Block (1919-) Chicago (N) (1942, 1945-46)	2B-3B	17	53	9	16	0	5	.302
Ron Blomberg (1948-) New York (A) (1969, 1971-76) Chicago (A) (1978)	DH-OF 1B	461	1333	184	391	52	224	.293
Sammy Bohne (1896-1977) St. Louis (N) (1916) Cincinnati (1921-26) Brooklyn (1926)	INF-OF	663	2315	309	605	16	228	.261
Lou Brower (1900-) Detroit (1931)	SS-2B	21	62	3	10	0	6	.161

Batters		G	AB	R	H	HR	RBI	AVG
Rod Carew (1945-) Minnesota (1967-78) California (1978-) (record through 1985)	INF-DH OF	2469	9315	1424	3053	92	1015	.328
Harry Chozen (1915-) Cincinnati (1937)	C	1	4	0	1	0	0	.250
Alta Cohen (1908-) Brooklyn (1931-32) Philadelphia (N) (1933)	OF	29	67	8	13	0	2	.194
Andy Cohen (1904-) New York (N) (1926, 1928-29)	2B-SS 3B	262	886	108	249	14	114	.281
Phil Cooney (1886-deceased) New York (A) (1905)	3B	1	3	0	0	0	0	.000
Harry Danning (1911-) New York (N) (1933-42)	C-1B	890	2971	363	847	57	397	.285
Ike Danning (1905-83) St. Louis (A) (1928)	C	2	6	0	3	0	1	.500
Mike Epstein (1943-) Baltimore (1966-67) Washington (1967-71) Oakland (1971-72) Texas (1973) California (1973-74)	1B	907	2854	362	695	130	380	.244
Reuben Ewing (1899-1970) St. Louis (N) (1921)	SS	3	1	0	0	0	0	.000
Al Federoff (1924-) Detroit (1951-52)	2B-SS	76	235	14	56	0	14	.238
Eddie Feinberg (1918-1986) Philadelphia (N) (1938-39)	SS-2B OF	16	38	2	7	0	0	.184
Murray Franklin (1914-78) Detroit (1941-42)	SS-2B 3B	61	164	25	43	2	16	.262
Milt Galatzer (1907-76) Cleveland (1933-36) Cincinnati (1939) (Pitcher: 1 game 0-0)	OF-1B P	251	717	105	192	1	57	.268
Joe Ginsberg (1926-) Detroit (1948, 1950-53) Cleveland (1953-54) Kansas City (1956) Baltimore (1956-60) Chicago (A) (1960-61) Boston (A) (1961) New York (N) (1962)	C	695	1716	168	414	20	182	.241
Jonah Goldman (1906-80) Cleveland (1928, 1930-31)	SS-3B	148	389	33	87	1	49	.224

Batters		G	AB	R	H	HR	RBI	AVG

Jake Goodman (1853-90)
    Milwaukee (N) (1878)
    Pittsburgh (AA) (1882)
	1B	70	293	33	75	1	NA	.256

Sid Gordon (1917-75)
    New York (N) (1941-43,
    1946-49, 1955)
    Boston (N) (1950-52)
    Milwaukee (N) (1953)
    Pittsburgh (1954-55)
	OF-3B
	1B-2B
		1475	4992	735	1415	202	805	.283

Herb Gorman (1924-53) St. Louis (N) (1952)	PH	1	1	0	0	0	0	.000

Hank Greenberg (1911-)
    Detroit (1930, 1933-41,
    1945-46)
    Pittsburgh (1947)
	1B-OF	1394	5193	1051	1628	331	1276	.313

Steve Hertz (1945-) Houston (1964)	3B	5	4	2	0	0	0	.000

Benny Kauff (1890-1961)
    New York (A) (1912)
    Indianapolis (F) (1914)
    Brooklyn (F) (1915)
    New York (N) (1916-20)
	OF	859	3094	521	961	49	454	.311

Johnny Kling (1875-1947)
    Chicago (N) (1900-08,
    1910-11)
    Boston (N) (1911-12)
    Cincinnati (1913)
	C-OF
	SS-3B
	Mgr.
	1B
		1260	4241	474	1152	20	513	.272

Jim Levey (1906-70) St. Louis (A) (1930-33)	SS	440	1632	162	375	11	140	.230

Lou Limmer (1925-)
    Philadelphia (A) (1951,
    1954)
	1B	209	530	66	107	19	62	.202

Elliott Maddox (1947-)
    Detroit (1970)
    Washington (1971)
    Texas (1972-73)
    New York (A) (1974-76)
    Baltimore (1977)
    New York (N) (1978-80)
	OF-INF
	DH
		1029	2843	360	742	18	234	.261

Sam Mayer (1893-1962)
    Washington (1915)
    (Pitcher: 1 game 0-0)
	OF-1B
	P
		11	29	5	7	1	4	.241

Norm Miller (1946-)
    Houston (1965-73)
    Atlanta (1973-74)
	OF-3B
	C
		540	1364	166	325	24	159	.238

Batters		G	AB	R	H	HR	RBI	AVG
ddy Myer (1904-74) Washington (1925-27, 1929-41) Boston (A) (1927-28)	2B-3B SS-OF	1923	7038	1174	2131	38	850	.303
lly Nash (1865-1929) Richmond (AA) (1884) Boston (N) (1885-89, 1891-95) Boston (P) (1890) Philadelphia (N) (1896-98) (Pitcher: 2 games 0-0)	3B-2B SS-P OF Mgr.	1549	5849	1072	1606	61	976	.275
ff Newman (1948-) Oakland (1976-82) Boston (A) (1983-84) (Pitcher: 1 game 0-0)	C-1B DH-3B 2B-P	735	2123	189	475	63	233	.224
y Pike (deceased) Hartford (N) (1877)	OF	1	4	0	1	0	0	.250
pman Pike (1845-93) Troy (NA) (1871) Lord Baltimore (NA) (1872-73) Hartford (NA) (1874) St. Louis (NA) (1875) St. Louis (N) (1876) Cincinnati (N) (1877-78) Providence (N) (1878) Worcester (N) (1881) New York (AA) (1887)	OF-INF Mgr.	National Association Totals						
		260	1254	303	402	NA	NA	.321
		Major League Totals						
		163	733	133	223	5	88	.304
ke Pitler (1894-1968) Pittsburgh (1917-18)	2B-OF	111	383	40	89	0	23	.232
nmy Reese (1904-) New York (A) (1930-31) St. Louis (N) (1932)	2B-3B	232	742	123	206	8	70	.278
l Richter (1927-) Boston (A) (1951, 1953)	SS	6	11	1	1	0	0	.091
hief Roseman (1856-1938) Troy (N) (1882) New York (AA) (1883-87) Philadelphia (AA) (1887) Brooklyn (AA) (1887) St. Louis (AA) (1890) Louisville (AA) (1890) (Pitcher: 4 games 0-1)	OF-1B P-Mgr.	681	2761	443	726	15	NA	.263
l Rosen (1924-) Cleveland (1947-56)	3B-INF OF	1044	3725	603	1063	192	717	.285

Batters		G	AB	R	H	HR	RBI	AVG
Goody Rosen (1912-) Brooklyn (1937-39, 1944-46) New York (N) (1946)	OF	551	1916	310	557	22	197	.291
Harry Rosenberg (1909-) New York (N) (1930)	OF	9	5	1	0	0	0	.000
Lou Rosenberg (1903-) Chicago (A) (1923)	2B	3	4	0	1	0	0	.250
Max Rosenfeld (1902-69) Brooklyn (1931-33)	OF	42	57	8	17	2	7	.298
Si Rosenthal (1903-69) *Boston (A) (1925-26)*	OF	123	357	40	95	4	42	.266
Mickey Rutner (1922-) Philadelphia (A) (1947)	3B	12	48	4	12	1	4	.250
Ike Samuels (1876-1942) St. Louis (N) (1895)	3B-SS	24	74	5	17	0	5	.230
Heinie Scheer (1900-76) Philadelphia (A) (1922-23)	2B-3B	120	345	36	73	6	33	.212
Richie Scheinblum (1942-) Cleveland (1965, 1967-69) Washington (1971) Kansas City (1972, 1974) Cincinnati (1973) California (1973-74) St. Louis (N) (1974)	OF-DH	462	1218	131	320	13	127	.263
Mike Schemer (1917-83) New York (N) (1945-46)	1B	32	109	10	36	1	10	.330
Art Shamsky (1941-) Cincinnati (1965-67) New York (N) (1968-71) Chicago (N) (1972) Oakland (1972)	OF-1B	665	1686	194	426	68	233	.253
Dick Sharon (1950-) Detroit (1973-74) San Diego (1975)	OF	242	467	46	102	13	46	.218
Norm Sherry (1931-) Los Angeles (N) (1959-62) New York (N) (1963)	C	194	497	45	107	18	69	.215
Al Silvera (1935-) Cincinnati (1955-56)	OF	14	7	3	1	0	2	.143
Mike Simon (1883-1963) Pittsburgh (1909-13) St. Louis (F) (1914) Brooklyn (F) (1915)	C	378	1069	·85	241	1	90	.225

Batters		G	AB	R	H	HR	RBI	AVG
red Sington (1910-) Washington (1934-37) Brooklyn (1938-39)	OF	181	516	66	140	7	85	.271
roadway Smith (1871-1919) Brooklyn (1897-1900) Baltimore (N) (1899) New York (N) (1901, 1906) Baltimore (A) (1902) Boston (A) 1903) Chicago (N) (1904)	C-OF 1B-2B 3B	287	955	107	252	1	130	.264
loe Solomon (1900-66) New York (N) (1923)	OF	2	8	0	3	0	1	.375
hick Starr (1911-) Washington (1935-36)	C	13	24	1	5	0	1	.208
an Stearns (1861-1944) Buffalo (N) (1880, 1885) Detroit (N) (1881) Cincinnati (AA) (1882) Baltimore (AA) (1883-85) Kansas City (AA) (1889)	1B-INF OF-C	509	2025	295	491	7	NA	.242
eorge Stone (1877-1945) Boston (A) (1903) St. Louis (A) (1905-10)	OF	848	3271	426	984	23	268	.301
e Strauss (1844-1906) Kansas City (U) (1884) Louisville (AA) (1885-86) Brooklyn (AA) (1886) (Pitcher: 2 games 0-0)	OF-C 2B-3B P	101	399	46	86	1	NA	.216
on Taussig (1932-) San Francisco (1958) St. Louis (N) (1961) Houston (1962)	OF	153	263	38	69	4	30	.262
ddie Turchin (1917-82) Cleveland (1943)	3B-SS	11	13	4	3	0	1	.231
hil Weintraub (1907-) New York (N) (1933-36, 1944-45) Cincinnati (1937) Philadelphia (N) (1938)	1B-OF	444	1382	215	407	32	207	.295

Pitchers		G	IP	SO	BB	W	L	ERA

Lloyd Allen (1950-)
  California (1969-73)
  Texas (1973-74)
  Chicago (A) (1974-75)
	R	159	297	194	196	8	25	4.70

Ross Baumgarten (1955-)
  Chicago (A) (1978-81)
  Pittsburgh (1982)
	L	90	496	222	211	22	36	3.99

Bo Belinsky (1936-)
  Los Angeles (A) (1962-64)
  Philadelphia (N) (1965-66)
  Houston (1967)
  Pittsburgh (1969)
  Cincinnati (1970)
	L	146	665	476	333	28	51	4.10

Conrad Cardinal (1942-) Houston (1963)	R	6	13	7	7	0	1	6.08
Hy Cohen (1931-) Chicago (N) (1955)	R	7	17	4	10	0	0	7.94

Sydney Cohen (1908-)
  Washington (1934,
    1936-37)
  (Outfield: 1 game)
	L	55	109	49	37	3	7	4.54

Richard Conger (1921-70)
  Detroit (1940)
  Pittsburgh (1941-42)
  Philadelphia (N) (1943)
	R	19	70	24	35	3	7	5.14

Harry Eisenstat (1915-)
  Brooklyn (1935-37)
  Detroit (1938-39)
  Cleveland (1939-42)
	L	165	478	157	114	25	27	3.84

Harry Feldman (1919-62) New York (N) (1941-46)	R	143	666	254	300	35	35	3.80
Julie Freeman (1868-1921) St. Louis (AA) (1888)		1	6	1	4	0	1	4.26
Izzy Goldstein (1908-) Detroit (1932)	R	16	56	14	41	3	2	4.47

Ken Holtzman (1945-)
  Chicago (N) (1965-71,
    1978-79)
  Oakland (1972-75)
  Baltimore (1976)
  New York (A) (1976-78)
	L	451	2867	1601	910	174	150	3.49

Herman Iburg (1877-1945) Philadelphia (N) (1902)	R	30	236	106	62	11	18	3.89

Harry Kane (1883-1932)
  St. Louis (A) (1902)
  Detroit (1903)
  Philadelphia (N) (1905-06)
	L	15	86	43	50	2	7	4.81

Pitchers		G	IP	SO	BB	W	L	ERA
Herb Karpel (1917-) New York (A) (1946)	L	2	1	0	0	0	0	10.80
Robert Katz (1911-62) Cincinnati (1944)	R	6	18	4	7	0	1	3.93
William Kling (1867-1934) Philadelphia (N) (1891) Baltimore (N) (1892) Louisville (N) (1895)	R	15	87	33	40	4	4	5.17
Alan Koch (1938-) Detroit (1963-64) Washington (1964)	R	42	128	73	55	4	11	5.41
Howie Koplitz (1938-) Detroit (1961-62) Washington (1964-66)	R	54	175	87	80	9	7	4.21
Sandy Koufax (1935-) Brooklyn (1955-57) Los Angeles (N) (1958-66)	L	397	2324	2396	817	165	87	2.76
Barry Latman (1936-) Chicago (A) (1957-59) Cleveland (1960-63) Los Angeles (A) (1964-65) Houston (1966-67)	R	344	1219	829	489	59	68	3.91
Duke Markell (1923-84) St. Louis (A) (1951)	R	5	21	10	20	1	1	6.33
Ed Mayer (1931-) Chicago (N) (1957-58)	L	22	31	17	18	2	2	4.31
Erskine Mayer (1891-1957) Philadelphia (N) (1912-18) Pittsburgh (1918-19) Chicago (A) (1919)	R	245	1427	482	345	91	70	2.96
Sam Nahem (1915-) Brooklyn (1938) St. Louis (N) (1941) Philadelphia (N) (1942, 1948)	R	90	224	101	127	10	8	4.69
Barney Pelty (1880-1939) St. Louis (A) (1903-12) Washington (1912)	R	266	1918	693	532	92	117	2.62
Steve Ratzer (1953-) Montreal (1980-81)	R	13	21	4	9	1	1	7.29
Ed Reulbach (1882-1961) Chicago (N) (1905-13) Brooklyn (N) (1913-14) Newark (F) (1915) Boston (N) (1916-17)	R	398	2632	1137	892	181	105	2.28

Pitchers		G	IP	SO	BB	W	L	ERA
Saul Rogovin (1922-) Detroit (1949-51) Chicago (A) (1951-53) Baltimore (1955) Philadelphia (N) (1955-57)	R	150	883	388	308	48	48	4.06
Marv Rotblatt (1927-) Chicago (A) (1948, 1950-51)	L	35	74	30	51	4	3	4.82
Moe Savransky (1929-) Cincinnati (1954)	L	16	24	7	8	0	2	4.88
Al Schacht (1892-1984) Washington (1919-21)	R	53	197	38	61	14	10	4.48
Sid Schacht (1918-) St. Louis (A) (1950-51) Boston (N) (1951)	R	19	21	12	21	0	2	14.34
Larry Sherry (1935-) Los Angeles (N) (1958-63) Detroit (1964-67) Houston (1967) California (A) (1968)	R	416	799	606	374	53	44	3.67
Harry Shuman (1916-) Pittsburgh (1942-43) Philadelphia (N) (1944)	R	30	50	10	20	0	0	4.44
Steve Stone (1947-) San Francisco (1971-72) Chicago (A) (1973, 1977-78) Chicago (N) (1974-76) Baltimore (1979-81)	R	320	1789	1065	716	107	93	3.96
Bud Swartz (1929-) St. Louis (A) (1947)	L	5	5	1	7	0	0	6.75
Ed Wineapple (1906-) Washington (1929)	L	1	4	1	3	0	0	4.50
Ralph Winegarner (1909-) Cleveland (1930, 1932, 1934-36) St. Louis (A) (1949) (3B-OF-1B-P: 136 games AB:185 H:51 HR:5 AVG: .276)	R	70	194	89	89	8	6	5.33
Larry Yellen (1943-) Houston (1963-64)	R	14	26	12	11	0	0	6.23

HALL OF FAME

HANK GREENBERG (1956)   SANDY KOUFAX (1972)

ABOUT THE AUTHOR

Erwin Lynn was born of Jewish parents who emigrated from Eastern Europe in the 1920s. His father, Henry, was from Kamen Kashirskiy in the Ukraine, while his mother, Gussie, arrived from Nowy Dwor, Poland. They both settled in New York City, where they married, and had two children, Erwin and his sister Joyce.

Lynn, a graduate of The City College of New York, is the author of the *Jewish Baseball Quiz* that has appeared in numerous Anglo-Jewish newspapers throughout the United States and Canada. He resides on Long Island with his wife Paula, and their three children, Cheryl, Jennifer, and Jason.

PHOTO CREDITS: Photographs were supplied by the baseball celebrities in this book except for the following: Morrie Arnovich, Dolly Stark, Al Rosen (pg. 77), Hank Greenberg, Andy Cohen, and Cal Abrams—all from the collection of Ted & Eleanor Mishanie; Erskine Mayer, Chief Roseman and Mike Simon—all from the collection of Lew Lipset; Harry Danning and Ike Danning—both from the collection of Mrs. Clifford Gross; George Stone, Johnny Kling, Jake Atz and the Cincinnati 1882 American Association Champions—all from the collection of Mark R. Schaffer; Steve Ratzer from the Montreal Expos Baseball Club; Steve Hertz from the Houston Astros Baseball Club; Ken Holtzman from the Oakland Athletics Baseball Club; Al Rosen from the San Francisco Giants Baseball Club; Sandy Koufax, © 1963 the Los Angeles Dodgers Baseball Club; Richie Scheinblum from the Cleveland Indians Baseball Club; Mike Epstein from the Baltimore Orioles Baseball Club; and the Cincinnati Reds 1940 World Champions from the Cincinnati Reds Baseball Club.

LEAGUE LEADERS

Batters

Batting Average

1906	George Stone, St. Louis (A)	.358
1935	Buddy Myer, Washington (A)	.349
1969	Rod Carew, Minnesota (A)	.332
1972	Rod Carew, Minnesota (A)	.318
1973	Rod Carew, Minnesota (A)	.350
1974	Rod Carew, Minnesota (A)	.364
1975	Rod Carew, Minnesota (A)	.359
1977	Rod Carew, Minnesota (A)	.388
1978	Rod Carew, Minnesota (A)	.333

Home Runs

1877	Lipman Pike, Cincinnati (N)	4
1938	Hank Greenberg, Detroit (A)	58
1940	Hank Greenberg, Detroit (A)	41
1946	Hank Greenberg, Detroit (A)	44
1950	Al Rosen, Cleveland (A)	37
1953	Al Rosen, Cleveland (A)	43

Runs-Batted-In

1935	Hank Greenberg, Detroit (A)	170
1937	Hank Greenberg, Detroit (A)	183
1940	Hank Greenberg, Detroit (A)	150
1946	Hank Greenberg, Detroit (A)	127
1952	Al Rosen, Cleveland (A)	105
1953	Al Rosen, Cleveland (A)	145

Pitchers

WINNING PERCENTAGE

		W-L	Pct.
1906	Ed Reulbach, Chicago (N)	19-4	.826
1907	Ed Reulbach, Chicago (N)	17-4	.810
1908	Ed Reulbach, Chicago (N)	24-7	.774
1964	Sandy Koufax, Los Angeles (N)	19-5	.792
1965	Sandy Koufax, Los Angeles (N)	26-8	.765
1980	Steve Stone, Baltimore (A)	25-7	.781

EARNED RUN AVERAGE

		IP	ERA
1951	Saul Rogovin, Detroit-Chicago (A)	217	2.78
1962	Sandy Koufax, Los Angeles (N)	184	2.54
1963	Sandy Koufax, Los Angeles (N)	311	1.88
1964	Sandy Koufax, Los Angeles (N)	223	1.74
1965	Sandy Koufax, Los Angeles (N)	336	2.04
1966	Sandy Koufax, Los Angeles (N)	323	1.73

STRIKEOUTS

1961	Sandy Koufax, Los Angeles (N)	269
1963	Sandy Koufax, Los Angeles (N)	306
1965	Sandy Koufax, Los Angeles (N)	382
1966	Sandy Koufax, Los Angeles (N)	317

NO-HITTERS

Bo Belinsky	1962
Sandy Koufax	1962, 1963 1964, 1965 (Perfect Game)
Ken Holtzman	1969, 1971

HALL OF FAME
HANK GREENBERG (1956)   SANDY KOUFAX (1971)